Dear Winston

I hope you _____ book as much as _____ it. I was a bit sad when it came to an end. But it is a rewarding experience to have the memories down in a book for family and others to enjoy. I feel honored and humbled to be an author. I give the praise and glory to God though for granting me good recall, and for giving me the zeal, enthusiasm, and fortitude to complete such a big endeavor.

New author,
Judith Kuipers Walhout

A FARM GIRL'S *Memories*

JUDITH KUIPERS WALHOUT

WESTBOW
P R E S S®
A DIVISION OF THOMAS NELSON
& ZONDERVAN

WestBow Press books may be ordered through booksellers or by contacting:

WestBow Press
A Division of Thomas Nelson & Zondervan
1663 Liberty Drive
Bloomington, IN 47403
www.westbowpress.com
1 (866) 928-1240

Scripture taken from the King James Version of the Bible.

Scripture quotations marked (NIV) are taken from the Holy Bible, New International Version®, NIV®. Copyright © 1973, 1978, 1984, 2011 by Biblica, Inc.® Used by permission of Zondervan. All rights reserved worldwide. www.zondervan.com The "NIV" and "New International Version" are trademarks registered in the United States Patent and Trademark Office by Biblica, Inc.®

ISBN: 978-1-9736-9379-6 (sc)
ISBN: 978-1-9736-9378-9 (e)

Print information available on the last page.

WestBow Press rev. date: 07/24/2020

DEDICATION

A few years ago, a good friend said to me, "You have a way with words. You should write a book." That was a surprise and sounded like a huge impossibility to me . . . I thought, why? What would I ever write about? However, that thought about writing a book kept popping up, nudging me to go ahead and do it. I kept thinking about this and wondering—-could I really do this? I decided maybe I had enough memories from growing up on our small farm, and that would be what I would like to share with others. I have always enjoyed reading books about peoples' pasts, their stories, and their childhood memories.

So, good friend, Linda Weeda, this book is dedicated to you, foremost, for putting an idea in my head that would not go away. You may not even remember that you said it to me, but I never forgot. If it was not for that one statement, this book would never have materialized. I would not have been prompted to do what I thought was an impossibility. Thanks, Linda, for hinting about this and making the suggestion!

Next, I also dedicate it to my four daughters, Kimberly, Kristi, Nichole, and Alicia whom I love very dearly, and thank them for their encouragement and for not saying it was an inconceivable idea. Also, thanks to my loving husband for letting me work on it freely whenever I wished. It has been interesting reliving all my memories on our farm, and I hope others will enjoy reading them.

My very special thanks to Nichole, Kim, and my friend, Renetta Brovont in Pennsylvania, for all their time in proofreading, suggestions, and correcting errors. That was so helpful, invaluable, beneficial, and supportive. I cannot thank you all enough! It was an exciting adventure and I enjoyed writing the stories and memories as they came flooding in. It was amazing how the different stories and events would surface in my mind when I least expected it, perhaps when lying in bed at night, or while traveling down the highway. They all were stored in my mind, since I never kept a journal. Some memories I needed to ask my sister and brothers about. I hope I remembered all the stories and happenings that I would have wanted to include! Knowing me, about four months after the book is printed, I will think of something I wish I had included.

Sometimes this task of organizing and getting my thoughts into print was a bit overwhelming. Other times I got going and could not quit. One night I could not fall asleep and so wrote most of a chapter from 11 p.m. until 1:15 in the morning. I feel it is a good time in my life to be doing this since I am now seventy-five years of age and as the years go by, my mind could begin to fail. So I am happy to be getting these memories, stories, and happenings down in written form. Mostly, it has been pleasurable and fulfilling writing it, and it was hard for me to quit and bring it to an end. It was like saying "good-bye" to a friend. It has been challenging, gratifying, interesting, rewarding, and an adventurous writing experience. I am thankful to be writing a book to pass on to my spouse, children, sons-in-law, grandchildren, extended family, friends, and hopefully many others who will enjoy and relish reading about the memories on our farm.

It is my heartfelt and sincere prayer that God will bless what I have written and use it to touch and influence some lives. May it impact parents in such a way that they will strive to be more worthy of the responsibility that God has given them when raising their precious children. May they 'press on' and ask for the Lord's help and guidance in raising God-fearing, respectable, honorable, moral, upright, and principled children. It is the family that needs to remain strong and be united to fight the battles, corruption, and depravity in the world today. I would like to end with a verse from the King James Version of the Bible. We read in 1 Corinthians 15:58, "Therefore, my beloved brethren, be ye steadfast, unmovable, always abounding in the work of the Lord, forasmuch as ye know that your labour is not in vain in the Lord." Then a final verse from the New International Version of the Bible, from Philippians 4:13, "I 'press on' toward the goal to win the prize for which God has called me heavenward in Christ Jesus." May God bless the words He laid on my heart to write, and may He bless the hearts and lives of those who read *A Farm Girl's Memories!*

Rothbury, Michigan Featured Families

Kuipers Grandparents: Fred G. Kuipers and Reintje DeVoss (10 children)

Andrew	Gerbic	
Clarence (my dad)	Anna —— Anna Kuipers and John Diepen	
Elizabeth	Henry	Angeline Diepen and Marinus Boer
Tjamke	Frank	Betty
Gertrude	Sena	Ron
		Linda

Clarence Kuipers and Elsie Fischer
- Elinor
- Donald
- Vernon
- Herbert
- Judith —— Judith Kuipers and Richard Walhout
  - Kimberly
- Darlene
  - Kristi
  - Nichole
  - Alicia

Fischer Grandparents: John Henry Fischer Sr. and Louise Elizabeth Schroeder
Carl
John Jr. (Pat)
Emma
Elsie (my mom)
William
Henry —— Henry Fischer and Dorothy Prill
- Glen
- Bruce
- Diane

Relatives in Bismarck, North Dakota: Gerbic (my dad's brother) and Emma Kuipers

Carl —— Carl and Betty Kuipers (eight children)
Vivian
John

CONTENTS

ANCESTORS, LOG CABIN, PARENTS

One beautiful summer day, my dad told me to cut some hay fields on our 80 acres. My brothers were already out of the house so my dad relied on me, his young teenage daughter, for help around the farm which included driving the tractor. The tractor we had was an Allis Chalmers WD tractor, and the mower had a long sickle blade. I had a lot of experience mowing, raking, and baling hay, so I went merrily down the road on my way to the hay fields on the "80". I can still envision the day. It was warm and sunny, birds were singing, honey bees humming as they flew from the purple alfalfa and clover blossoms to the next blossoms, grasshoppers hopping on the hay stalks, insects flying about, and a rabbit hiding here and there. I arrived at the first field, got off the tractor, lowered the blade, hopped back on the tractor, and went to work.

I was always very particular and liked to do things well, getting all the hay mowed down without missing many stalks. If I missed a small patch, I would usually turn around and mow it down. This specific field, which I had mowed many times before, had a stump near the edge of the field with many leafy branches growing out of it totally covering the stump. I always thought the stump was located more in the middle of all the branches and got close to do my thorough job. But I was wrong! It was close to the edge, but hidden, and as I mowed up to it, I nicked it with the tractor's left back wheel when going around it. That in itself would have been okay, but this was also on a small side hill so when I nicked the stump just right, I tipped the tractor over. Now this happened sixty some years ago, so I cannot remember if it totally tipped over, but I think the tractor landed on its side. My leg was pinned underneath the right fender, and the tractor was still running, as well as the mowing machine. My first thought was, I am going to get hit with the mower blade and lose an arm or a leg! Thankfully, after several tries, I was able to pull my leg free and scramble away. I could see I was in no danger and could reach under and shut the tractor off, which also shut the mower off. I thought, "Now what?"—no cell phones back then! I was rather shaken up, but I did not want to go to the closest house to call my dad. I chose instead to walk to my uncle and aunt's house half a mile up the road. Uncle Henry was home, so he drove back to the tractor to make sure things were all right there. He tried to make me feel better about tipping over the tractor. The mower blade was badly bent and curved so he said, "No problem—now it would cut in the valleys better!" Then he brought me home. My leg hurt quite badly and was swollen where the tractor had hit it. It hit on the inside of my leg, a bit up from my ankle. After awhile, my mom decided to have a doctor check it out. Nothing was broken, but I had a lump and scar from that accident for years. I still know exactly where my leg was hit. My brother also had tipped over that same tractor several times being the front wheels were close together, making it easier to tip over. I was very apprehensive to get back on the tractor after tipping it over, but my dad said the best thing to do was to get right back on and continue with my job of tractor driving. So after a few days, I gathered my courage, bravely climbed back onto the seat, and continued my work as a tractor operator. Soon after my accident, my dad got a tractor with a wide front end and with the wheels far apart. We never tipped the tractor over again after that.

Here, then, is how it came about that I would drive tractor on a small farm five miles southeast of New Era, Michigan. My grandpa on my father's side, Fred G. Kuipers, left Amsterdam, Holland in 1890, hoping for a better life, first settling in Chicago. He had left his girlfriend, Reintje DeVoss, in the Netherlands, and after working in Chicago for a year, he sent for her. They were married and had two children while living in Chicago. In 1895 they moved to Michigan, staying with friends and their family. Later, he bought property and built a log cabin on it, where five more children were born. In 1904, he bought forty acres of land east of Rothbury, which was not far at all from the log cabin, and built a new home there. My dad was born in 1903. After my dad, three more children came, making ten children (though one died at five months). This home that has been remodeled several times, still has some of the first, older foundation. The house stands there on the property yet, as well as the original barn and garage. The Kuipers' home and outbuildings on the 40 acres have remained in the Kuipers' family to this day. A niece, my brother Herb's daughter, bought the farm when my mom passed away in 1998.

My grandpa from my mother's side, John Fischer, came from Bavaria, Germany when he was only a teenager. I recently asked my ninety-nine year old aunt about this, and she said he came over at the age of fifteen. Since he was approaching the age of mandatory enlistment for three years in the military and would have to be in the reserves for another three years, he booked passage for $35.00 and came to America. He joined two of his sisters in Chicago. He left his dad, who was a successful horticulturist, and a younger brother, Leonard, in Germany. His mother had passed away giving birth to Leonard. His dad, Johann Thomas Fischer, and Leonard came when they could, and in 1892 he also purchased land east of Rothbury, Michigan. This farm was one and a quarter miles up the road from the Kuipers' farm.

There used to be native white pine on it, but it had been lumbered off. Great-grandpa used his green thumb and raised berry bushes and sold starts to others living around him. He had some cattle as well and raised some other crops. My grandpa married Louise Elizabeth Schroeder in 1901 and eventually took over this farm. Later cherries, asparagus, bushes, trees and seedlings were raised and became Fischer Trees. This farm has remained in the Fischer family ever since. They had eight children and one became my mother, but two girls died in infancy.

My dad, Clarence Kuipers, and my mother, Elsie Fischer, were married June 8, 1929 and settled thirty miles away in the town of Muskegon. Five of their children were born in Muskegon (one baby died). In 1946 they moved back to the 40 acre farm where my dad grew up, and at some point the 80 acres located a mile up the road were added to the farm. Dad loved farming and animals and hoped to make a living at it. Another daughter was born in 1948. Unable, though, to make a suitable living from the farm, Dad went back to work in Muskegon at Continental Motors. He had to drive this thirty mile trip back and forth for many years. He kept up the farm too, and had some milk cows, beef cattle, chickens, pigs, a horse now and then, and of course always cats and a dog. This small farm is where I grew up and I will share some of those memories.

When thinking of these ancestors on both sides of the family, they did well in their move to America. They had some tough times, but by working hard managed with what little they had. They instilled good morals and values in their children, taught them faith in God, integrity, and respect for others.

My dad attended a one room school, and as many did back then, only completed the eighth grade. When he got older, he spent a summer out west with the grain harvesters working with large teams of horses. Upon returning to Michigan, he married my mom and they were married for fifty-eight years! My oldest sister said when the roads were too muddy, my folks would go to church by horse and buggy so they could get through the mud better. So, I do not know when they purchased their first car. But when thinking about it, what great changes in that generation were witnessed by my parents and others: from horse and buggy to cars, radios to televisions, airplanes, microwaves, and everyone having a telephone in their homes.

Things special about my dad were his genuine smile and friendliness. He was interested in others and loved life in general. He was a real handyman, and you could often find him in the garage repairing something. He had a good mind and kept up with current events, news, and sports. He could get pretty excited when watching baseball on TV. When we had problems with homework, even in high school, he would help us even though he only went through the 8th grade himself. He was always willing to do his best and instilled this in his children also. He enjoyed gardening and I got my love for gardening from him. Riding around the countryside looking at the farms was a favorite thing dad liked to do, and taking Sunday afternoon drives down two-track roads. So when I think of Dad, I think about his pleasant disposition and how he delighted in visiting with anyone. He was so good at always complimenting my mom on her delicious meals or baked goods (of course, she was a very excellent cook and baker!). A thing of interest was when my folks were visiting my sister in California. They went to see one of their favorite shows "Joker's Wild" being filmed. And to everyone's surprise, my dad was actually picked to be a contestant on the show! He lost, but I was very proud of the good, logical answer he gave about losing. He was asked if he felt bad about losing. His quick reply was he did not feel too bad about losing since it really was not his in the first place. He got a big round of applause from the audience.

Dad taught me lots of things . . . how to play Pinochle and Pedro, two of his favorite card games. My two brothers were soon out of the house: the oldest married, and the next brother working on a farm ten miles away to earn money. So Dad would have me help considerably on the farm, and I did a lot of tractor work! He taught me to cut hay, rake hay, bale hay, cultivate corn, and drag. He also taught me to drive a pick-up truck with a stick shift at a young age. He was a patient teacher and taught me well.

Another thing about Dad, he did not do the disciplining of us girls very often. It was usually Mom who bawled us out, sent us to our room, or grabbed and squeezed our upper arm quite hard. Or maybe a couple times my mouth got washed out with soap for saying something inappropriate. Maybe not the healthiest thing to do, but I certainly remembered and never repeated something bad again! This one time, however, Dad spanked me hard with a hairbrush, and it hurt! He spanked me for spilling Mom's perfume when I did not do it. I think it accidentally got spilled when someone got a towel out of the cupboard, but everyone got blamed for it.

One of my favorite memories of my father is when he would watch Lassie on TV with my younger sister and me, and tears would come down his cheeks too. We thought that was all right for him to show emotion. I always remember him playing Pinochle and Pedro and the fun he had; he was very good at it too! My parents often had couples over or went to their homes to play cards, especially Pinochle. When Dad was retired, a widow lady friend would come over, and the three of them would sit playing cards until the wee hours of the morning . . . two a.m. sometimes! I liked watching and listening to Dad when he was visiting with others; he so enjoyed having company and visiting. One other thing . . . my sister and I would get such a kick out of watching Dad trying to read his newspaper. He would get so sleepy, and the papers kept falling down lower and lower in his lap until they made a noise. Then he would wake up, pick up the newspaper, only to again soon be dozing, and the process would start all over again many, many times.

My mother, born in 1908, also grew up on a farm, and when she was a teenager went to Chicago to work. She worked for a dentist doing the cleaning and cooking. There she got free dental care and some real, gold fillings. Mom often told about her great love of ice skating, and how she and her siblings would traipse a good mile or so across the fields to a lake behind their property to skate. Also, they would play and skate on a small pond by their one room schoolhouse where she attended through the eighth grade. She often mentioned that two children had drowned in that pond!

Some of my favorite memories of my mom were her laughter and that she loved to tease and play jokes. I remember when she was dressed up to go some place with Dad, she looked so pretty and smelled so nice when I kissed her good-bye. She was always the gracious hostess when we had company and was so good at making guests feel at home. She always made sure they had plenty to eat! I remember Mom and Dad sitting on the couch holding hands, showing deep love and respect in their marriage. She was always bringing meals and baked goods to the elderly, sick, pastors, or newcomers; she cared for others. She liked using little sayings and often told us, "Do unto others as you would have them do unto you." Or, "If you can't say anything nice . . . don't say anything at all." One she would say in German and it meant, "If you laugh too much and are too silly, soon you will wind up crying."

Now, a few incidents telling of Mom's humor and fun in life . . . when she was about fifty-seven years old, she and a friend of mine dressed up (putting panty hose over their faces, looking really weird), and they went trick-or-treating to the neighbors. I was college age and went along but was the driver. And the story of when Dad and Mom were at the grocery store, and she saw some empty boxes the stock boy had left. She decided to step in them and walk around in them for a while to be funny. My dad quickly walked away and pretended he did not know her. When her company would sit down at the table to eat, they often found a huge spoon or fork or something out of place at their spot at the table. One meal time my sister's friend told my mom that she was not a "very big potato" eater to which my mom promptly replied, "No problem, these were all small potatoes." Or, if she was serving pie or cake and the guests would say just a small piece, she would cut it so tiny you could hardly see it.

Mom really looked forward to April Fool's day. I think she thought long and hard ahead of time what tricks to pull on her husband and children. Maybe one of the best was when Mom hollered up the stairs in the wee hours of the morning to my brother and me, asleep in our bedrooms. She hollered to hurry, get up, and get dressed as the cows were out, and we needed to round them up and get them back in their fenced-in pasture. Being the obedient child that I was, I quickly responded and was half dressed, when my brother shouted from his room and told me to go back to sleep; it was just an April Fool's joke.

My mom truly loved to cook and bake, and she was very, very good at it! Oh, what tantalizing and savory smells embraced us from the kitchen when we would come in from the cold outdoors! When my sister and I were older, we often helped with the cleaning so she could devote her time to baking on Saturdays. The table and kitchen counter would have an array of her baked goods. Often you could see six coffee cakes, homemade rolls, a couple of pies, and maybe some cookies, or a cake on display. She made such tasty pies: apple, cherry, lemon, pecan, peanut butter, graham cracker, raisin cream, and Dad liked mincemeat pie (not me), to name a few. To explain, mincemeat pie had a mixture of minced apples, maybe suet, and sometimes meat along with raisins and currants and everything was cut up very small, thus called mincemeat pie. I think her pies were so delicious because she used her own homemade lard. This lard was made from the fat of a pig and rendered, or boiled for a long time to separate impurities. The lard made the crust so light and flaky . . . very tasty!

Also high on the list of delicacies were her homemade overnight rolls, bread pudding, German Chocolate cake, and

Angel Food cake (and not box mixes), cookies and bars, and homemade bread and doughnuts. When my girls got older, they loved going out to help Grandma and Grandpa make homemade doughnuts. They would make a lot of them, and the glazed ones were hung on carrom sticks, set on six inch blocks of wood to dry.

Often we could find Mom working on crossword puzzles and word searches, something she also enjoyed. She could play piano some, and I think she just picked it up on her own never having any lessons. Later in life, when her memory was failing, it was amazing how she could sit at the piano or old pump organ we had and still play some hymns by memory. We are privileged to own that antique organ and have it in our home now.

From my mother, I learned how to bake, sew, garden, grow flowers, and how to be a good mother, wife, and homemaker. I did not ever attain her level of skills for cooking and baking, however. I was always doing outdoor work and tractor work, so I did not spend enough time with her inside. But she taught us to be polite and use good manners and always to say please and thank you. When grandchildren came along, she always made sure they said please and thank you also. She taught us respect, honor, kindness and to be helpful and caring. Because she always worked hard, she taught me to be a good worker, to take pride in doing things well. She often would say, "Do the best you can," and I often would say that to my children also. She had a great love for her family and tried hard for us to have a happy home. By her example, she taught us to delight and be happy in the little things and to be content.

Our parents raised us in the Christian faith and taught us the importance of faithful church attendance. They always made sure we went to church twice on Sundays (they went with us, of course), went to Sunday school, and to catechism—these things were priorities in our lives. So we would go to Sunday school in the morning and turn around and go in the afternoons too. Some men from our church had an outreach ministry at our one room schoolhouse trying to reach the community kids, so we attended also. Our parents taught us what is important in life—God, church, and family. We were taught perseverance and to always put in a good day's work. And they taught us to be happy and content with what we have and where we are. They also taught us to be kind, loving, caring, polite, honest, fair, respectful, and to always do what is right. I use this last principle often when making decisions knowing 'it is the right thing to do.'

My mom laughed a lot and tried to get others to smile and laugh. My cousin, Carl Kuipers, wrote this about coming to visit at the Kuipers' farm; "We stayed with Aunt Elsie and Uncle Clarence, and I never saw anyone get so excited during a hot game of Pinochle as Uncle Clarence. I was afraid he was going to have a heart attack! Some of my best memories happened in your parents' home. Playing the old pump organ, sleeping upstairs, sitting in the screened-in porch, checking out the barn, going to the tree lot on the 80 acres—all those evergreens—making peanut butter pie with your mom, having fresh raspberries from their patch, and enjoying your mother's sense of humor. When she got the giggles, you could not help but laugh. She made everyone happy to be around her."

Carl mentioned about sitting in our screened-in porch. It was a nice place to sit and relax with a couple of comfortable chairs and a large glider where you could gently swing. The floor was covered with indoor outdoor carpeting. The road that went by the front of the house was not heavily traveled, so it was very peaceful to sit out on the porch. Dad had a large speaker for listening to the radio or music. When I sat out there, I liked listening to nature the best. During the daytime, birds would be singing and bees humming as they went from flower to flower. And evenings, the lovely sounds of frogs singing and other neat night sounds. Yes, it was a delightful and pleasant place to sit . . . anytime of the day. It was a large front porch too, so we often sat out there Sunday afternoons when we had company.

We were thankful that both Dad and Mom lived long and full lives. Dad made it to eighty-four years old before he died, and Mom lived to be ninety years old. They both came from large families, and life was not always easy for them. They had to work hard, but the ideals and morals that they passed on were invaluable! We tried to instill them in our children and now in our grandchildren also. My folks got them from their parents and from God's Word, and are as applicable today as they were when they were growing up and when we were growing up. Another thing, even in Mom's later years when her memory failed her, she never lost her sense of humor and still loved to tease. She really had a knack for trying to boost up people's spirits and that is how many people remember her . . . that she laughed a lot and tried to get others to smile and laugh. It would be nice if more of us had this attribute of being fun-loving, happy, and caring for other individuals. It could be a goal to be pleasant, kind, and work hard at making others happy also. So, I am thankful to my parents for those precious values and morals that they passed down to us and to our children too. It shows that if we put our faith and trust in God, He is faithful from one generation to the next generation.

SIBLINGS, 1944, VERY EARLIEST MEMORIES

I was born into a family of six children, though one brother passed away as an infant. My oldest sister, Elinor, was born in 1930 and was married in the farm house in 1950. Since I was not quite six when she married, I have very few recollections of my big sister when she was still living at home. I remember liking to climb in her bed with her upstairs sometimes. I also remember running outside to greet her when she came in the driveway from working. She drove an old car with running boards. I would hop up on them before she got out of the car to see if she brought me any treats of candy or other surprises. At that young age, she was pretty special to me.

Next was my brother Donald, born in 1934 and ten years older than me. Again, since he was a lot older, I do not have a lot of memories of Don growing up. I remember him helping Dad a lot on the farm. I have a brief memory of him and his girlfriend (who he married) at our house babysitting us once. The best thing, though, was when he was going to get married in 1953, and they asked my sister and me to be in the wedding. Darlene, at four, was going to be the flower girl along with a cousin, the ring bearer. I was eight at the time and going to be a very young junior bridesmaid. So, of course, we were going to wear fancy dresses for the occasion, and my sister-in-law-to-be also bought us new undies, slips, shoes, and socks. She tried them on us, and I remember being so excited to get all these brand new things, my sister and I were dancing and jumping all around in the living room with our new under things on. Must be that was an unusual occurrence to get new undies.

Vernon, who died at four months, was born in 1937; Mom told me he died of whooping cough. My brother, Herb, three years older than me came in 1941. I know he did not like me tagging along with him and his friends. But we did play some together, and as we got older, did chores and worked together. One special thing about Herb is when he bought a riding horse, Red. I used to beg and beg my parents for a horse but that just did not happen. Then when Herb was working out on another farm to earn money, he decided to buy a horse and kept it in our barn. He said if I would take care of it, I could ride it any time I wanted (I was in the 8th or 9th grade). It was just like owning my own horse as Herb rode it very few times the whole time we had Red. My wish of having a horse finally came true and I rode that horse a lot! He was a great horse. I could pull back on the reins and he would rear up some, just like the Lone Ranger on Silver.

I was born December 1, 1944 and then came my younger sister, Darlene, in 1948. I have one very early memory of when she was a baby and I do not even know if it is true or not, as my siblings do not recall it. I remember her being on the changing table and Mom had stepped out of the room a minute. I wanted to see Darlene better so I climbed up on the changing table and tipped her over, and me as well. Once I had a dream and wound up climbing in the crib with her. That triggers a memory of when I was still sleeping in a crib and old enough to be in a larger bed. I would hang my legs out of the bottom of the crib and tell Mom I was just too big for the crib!

When I was born in 1944, the President was Franklin D. Roosevelt and the Vice President was Henry Wallace. The world's population was 138,397,345, and a first class stamp was three cents. The popular movies were *Going My Way* with Bing Crosby, *National Velvet*, and *Meet Me In St. Louis* with Judy Garland. A gallon of gas was only fifteen cents, a loaf of bread nine cents, Campbell's tomato soup nine cents a can, minimum wage thirty cents an hour, and milk sixty-two cents a gallon. George Lucas, who created Star Wars, was born May 14, 1944, and Frank Sinatra began his film career. Pensive was the winner of the Kentucky Derby. Top songs were "San Fernando Valley" and "Swinging On a Star" (both Bing Crosby), and "Have Yourself a Merry Little Christmas" (Hugh Martin/Ralph Bline). Howard Hughes broke the U.S. transcontinental speed record in a Lockheed Constellation in April 1944. So that gives you a little idea of some happenings in 1944.

Now, a few more of my very, very earliest memories. I remember being just a little tyke and running around in the wind with a scarf on. That was popular in those days for girls to wear a scarf over the head, tied under the chin, to keep their ears warm. I can remember being in the backyard by the cement steps playing with some little cousins. I also remember a little about the first time I went to our one room schoolhouse in the country. I sat at my desk, swinging my feet, and was so proud to be in school. I would have been four when I started Kindergarten, as the cut off date then was December 5th, and I was born December 1st. At a young age, I really liked school.

Then, when I was still little, I remember being so excited when the big threshing machine came to thresh the grain. It would park in our driveway between the house and barn, and it was so, so big and noisy! Quite a crew would come to help thresh the wheat and oats, sometimes rye, and my mom would always work very hard to have a wonderful, huge lunch ready for the workers. She loved to cook, so would really go all out and would have several of her homemade pies baked too. My sister and I would stand around watching all this busy, bustling activity.

When older, we would go to catechism classes at our church in New Era, five miles away. We often carpooled with my cousins who lived just down the road from us. This happened on Saturday mornings, and each and every Saturday my mom would give us five cents to put in the collection at catechism and five cents to get an ice cream cone. There was a nice ice cream shop down on the corner a block from the church. A single dip cone was five cents and double dip was ten cents; on occasion we would get a treat and get ten cents for the double dip.

Some of my best memories were the fun and laughter when the whole family got together on Sunday afternoons. Both my married sister and married brother lived in New Era. Sometimes they joined us for Sunday dinner, and they almost always came out to visit on Sunday afternoons. There was always a lot of pleasant visiting, laughing, good times, and often they would stay for supper. Those Sunday night suppers were the best! My folks would stick a small ham in the oven and serve it sliced on my mom's homemade buns. Along with this, maybe a salad and an array of her famous baked goods. Sometimes in the afternoon, we'd set up the croquet set, and it was always fun playing that as a family when we were older. When brother Herb got married in 1963, they lived farther away as he became a Michigan State Policeman and had to settle where they assigned him. During his career they lived in New Buffalo, Ypsilanti, Battle Creek, and retired out of the Grand Haven post when he was forty-seven years old. Since they lived too far away, we did not see them as much. They would come, though, and spend a weekend every so often, and we would go to their house to see them too.

An unusual thing happened one of those Sunday afternoons when the family came out to visit. My older sister's daughter, Sharon, was learning to drive, so they let her practice improving her skills this particular Sunday afternoon. When they got to our second driveway, she was going a bit too fast to make the turn and tipped their Mustang right over on its side in the ditch. We all watched this happen from our big picture window in the living room. My sister, Darlene, almost fainted. Neighbors down the road saw it happen too and came up. My brother-in-law landed on Sharon, and my sister in the back seat squashed their other little daughter when landing on her. No one was hurt. It was a smaller car, so they either righted it with many hands or used the tractor to help get it back on all four wheels. It was a story often referred to in years to come, always causing a chuckle and often embarrassing my niece. Some did not think it was funny, though, when it happened.

This leads to another memory of a frightful accident. Grandpa Fischer, from up the road one and a quarter mile, was visiting. When it was time to run him back home, Mom had my brother, sister, and I ride along. We were too young to stay alone, and Dad probably was at work. Anyway, Grandpa sat in front with Mom, and we three kids were to get in the back. Darlene fussed and wanted to sit by the door so my mom let her, and Herb climbed in the middle. We were halfway to Grandpa's when all of a sudden there was a loud whoosh, and Darlene fell out of the moving car; she had gotten the door open. Grandpa was the first one back to check on her, and she was bleeding very badly from a gash on the top of her head. We proceeded to his house where Mom cleaned the wound at the kitchen sink. She finally was successful in getting the bleeding to stop and must have figured it was not too serious since we never took her to the doctor. Always after that, there was a vivid reminder of the accident because Darlene's doll, with a cloth body, had blood on it. She was never given a new doll to replace it.

We each only had one doll from little on. In fact, we had very few toys . . . for sure not like the abundance of toys kids have nowadays! We each had our dolls (mine was named Nancy and Darlene's was Mary), a few clothes with them, a small ironing board and iron, a teddy bear, some play dishes that were stored in a beautiful, blue wooden box, games, a Slinky, books, and not too much else. Dad did a nice thing for us and partitioned off the end of the attic with a window for a playhouse for us. It had an old couch in it and a table; we would play up there for hours. Often wasps joined us, buzzing around while we were playing. I remember having a wagon, and we used to play outdoors a lot. We often played back and forth with our cousins since they lived close by. Ron was Darlene's age and Betty two years younger than me. We rarely played inside; there were so many fun things to do outdoors like playing in the barn, playing games, making up things to play, climbing trees, and many other things. I agree with the saying, "Those were the good ol' days!"

MY HOUSE, BUTCHERING, LAUNDRY

I really liked growing up in the country and thoroughly enjoyed living on the farm! Our house was a two story home with two bedrooms upstairs and two bedrooms downstairs: my parents' room and a very small bedroom. There was only one bathroom which was common back then. The kitchen was huge as well as a good-sized living room and a large front room, which used to have french doors so it could be closed off. This front room was saved for special guests or a larger number of people, so we spent most of our time in the living room or in the kitchen. There was plenty of room when we had guests. I was proud of our house and of my folks and was eager to bring friends over to play, to spend a Sunday afternoon, or to spend the night. I even brought college friends home from Grand Rapids occasionally.

My favorite place in our home was my bedroom. When my sister, Darlene, and I were little, we shared a bed in the tiny room downstairs that much later was made into a laundry room. As older siblings got married and moved out, first I was able to take over the north bedroom upstairs. When Herb married, Darlene could then occupy the south bedroom upstairs. I always kept my room spotless and was pretty possessive of it! Since I was so particular with my room, I disliked it when my aunt Tillie visited from Chicago and had to use my bedroom. Well, I would not have minded just my aunt using the room, but her little ratty dog, Booty Boy, would stay up there too. We were not used to having animals in the house. We would not spend a lot of time upstairs during the winters since the rooms could be very cold with only one register between the two rooms. Also, it could get very hot upstairs in the summers and no air-conditioning.

I always cleaned my room very particularly each and every Saturday, including changing the sheets on the bed. One time I got the idea that I did not wish to mess up my sparkling clean room, so I decided to sleep in the barn at night. I thought it sounded like a fun thing to do, but it was not! I got very little sleep with cats coming to visit me, noises like mice scurrying around on the hay bales, maybe bats flying around, and who knows what other creepy, crawling things were climbing around beside me where I was trying to sleep. I did not give up, though, and stayed there the whole night.

Always keeping the house, lawns, vegetable garden, and flower beds looking very nice was a priority for my folks. We were taught at a young age to pitch in and help, especially working in the very large garden. We had our own chores to do. My chores, maybe from about fourth grade on, were sweeping the front and back porches on Saturdays, and sweeping out the large shed where we entered the house. Also, I fed and watered the chickens and gathered the eggs. I liked taking care of the chickens, though I was afraid of getting pecked when I gathered the eggs (which could happen sometimes). It was a bit of a stinky job, but I thought nothing of it. At some point, we started receiving a little chore money which was twenty-five cents a week.

My parents were always busy when we were growing up. Mom helped in the garden, fixed good and large meals, kept the house clean, sewed and baked, froze and canned lots of produce and meats, was a 4-H Leader, and she belonged to a Bible study with neighbor ladies (and to one with ladies at Church). We used to raise our own meat (a pig and sometimes beef also), which Dad and brother, Don, had to butcher. My brother, Herb, says he can remember one time (when he was not supposed to see it), when he saw them put a bushel basket over the pig's head and cut its throat. It was then hung by the barn door as it bled out. Then they fired up a big cast iron kettle, got the water boiling, put the pig in and scraped the hair off. I remember watching this step some. The big process of cutting up the meat was done on the kitchen table with both Dad and Mom working on this. Nothing would go to waste and parts that you maybe did not want to eat (like part of the pig's head), went into what was called headcheese. They sliced this meat which was a jelly-like consistency and often ate it on a slice of bread. We as kids never liked or ate any of this headcheese. Headcheese then was not a dairy cheese, but instead, was a meat made from what you could salvage from the pig's head. The head had to be simmered for a long time before you worked on it.

They would also eat the tongue and liver, and a snack we liked was "crackling" or pork rind. Mom fried the skin from the pig to make these tasty snacks. I saw that you can still buy these all prepared in bags in some stores. This butchering process was a lot of work! They did this when I was little, but later years they took the animal to get butchered at a butcher shop, or a neighbor a few miles up the road would come to help as butchering was his business. My folks had a huge freezer in the basement to put lots of meat and other goods in. Also, Mom would can a lot of meat, and we just loved this meat. It was always so tasty and tender, a real treat when we had it. Since it was easy to prepare (just open the lid and heat it up on the stove), that is what we often would fix when our parents were gone at supper time.

My mom would be very busy canning many, many things during the summers. Not only did she can vegetables from the huge garden, they would also buy a bushel or more of apples, peaches, pears, as well as some plums, prunes, and apricots. Also, there would be the blueberries, raspberries, and cherries to can. I even remember her canning sauerkraut, which is a German dish served with sausage. They raised their own cabbages, so would have chopped them up raw and pickled it in brine, making the sauerkraut before canning it. Pickles, too, were canned, and we would see them soaking for days in the two laundry tubs in the basement. Along with the freezer in the basement were many shelves on three walls of this room where Mom stored all her canned goods. Oh, also homemade applesauce and grape juice were made. We had our own row of grapes too, and that always produced a good supply of grapes. That was the best grape juice ever, and we so enjoyed it with popcorn. My mother was proud of her display of canned goods and often took company on a tour of that room. She should have been proud as it was a lot of hard work! We then had delicious canned goods to supplement our meals throughout the winters. I learned some canning techniques in home economics class in high school, but most of the art of canning came from my mom instructing me and showing me how. In my early years of marriage I would can tomatoes and pickles from my garden, can peaches and pears, and get grapes from my folks to make the delicious grape juice.

They also would butcher some chickens each year, maybe fifteen to twenty at a time. My dad had a chopping block for this purpose. Sometimes we would see Dad use the ax and block and watch the poor chicken flutter around without its head. All a part of growing up on the farm! After Dad's ax job, it was my mom's turn to take over. All the chickens were brought down to the basement where an old wood burning range was set up. It often came in handy when the power went out. It was good for warmth and for cooking when needed. It had at least four burners and an oven. Mom also did her laundry down in the basement and could light a fire in the range to take the chill off on the coldest winter days. Now back to the chickens. Mom would first pluck the feathers off the chickens, then use a fire in the range to singe off any remaining light 'hairy feathers.' Next, into the two laundry tubs they would go to get thoroughly washed. There was a table down there where Mom could cut them up. I remember playing with those chickens with my younger sister—in the laundry tubs or on the table: naked chickens with their necks, legs, and wings still on. We would grab them by their wings and try to make them sit up or dance them around. I guess we had to find something to amuse us while Mom was keeping an eye on us, when she was so busy with all her work. Those were really nice, plump chickens that Mom would make so delicious for a meal!

Every Monday was wash day on the farm and quite a big process. And for some reason it *ALWAYS* had to be on Monday; neighbors always did it on Monday also. For many years, my mom used a wringer washer down in the basement. First, she would sort the clothes in large piles on the basement floor. Then, load by load, they got done in the washer. First, all the sheets, pillowcases and hankies; next many towels, washcloths, dish towels, and dishrags; then, other articles of clothing; and always last were the boys' jeans and Dad's coveralls. Often, when doing a large washing, she would have to change the water halfway through if it got too dirty. From the washer, all the clothes had to be fed through the wringer into the first laundry tub, with 'bluing' added to it. This liquid bluing was a must as it was thought to keep the white fabrics whiter. In this first tub, the clothing got swished around and then run through the wringer again to the final rinse in the last laundry tub. When Darlene and I got older, we could help feed the clothes through the wringer. There was an art to this to make sure you did not get the clothes, or a hand caught in the wringer. Next, one more time through the wringer and piled into the basket to be carted up the stairs to the back yard.

Mom would hang the clothes on many lines outdoors to dry. There was a little pride, maybe, hanging them orderly with all towels together, socks, pillowcases, and so on. A lot of work, but there was nothing like the nice smelling towels, sheets, and pillowcases from being dried in the fresh air. When we got older, Darlene and I would help hang things if we were not busy doing something else. Finally, Dad made that back breaking job of hanging up a lot of clothes a bit easier. He used the bottom of an old lawn mower with the handle still on, and built a table on it just the right height so Mom did not have to bend over all the time when taking the clothes out of the basket. If it was raining or during wintertime, there were lines in the basement strung across the ceiling where the clothes could be hung to dry.

But alas, that was not the end to the laundry day. All the clothes had to be brought into the house when dry to be folded, and the things that needed to be ironed were lightly sprinkled and put in the refrigerator or freezer (until they were ironed). There was a lot of ironing in those days! For a long time, Mom even had a 'mangle' which was electric and used on large items like sheets, table cloths, towels, and other flat articles. It consisted of a rotating padded drum which revolved against a heating element. People used mangles since they pressed the larger items much faster than with an iron. Those that got real skilled at it, like my mom, could even iron men's shirts with it. I never acquired that skill, but I could do the sheets, tablecloths, and pillowcases. You fed the clothes into this big wide turning roller and the wrinkled clothes would emerge flat and pressed, without wrinkles when you did it right. This was a nice white machine with a cover that could be closed and stored right in the kitchen. My mom got rid of this when it was not needed as much anymore. Sheets finally were made with better materials so were more wrinkle-free. And dryers helped get wrinkles out of a lot of clothes also. Later, Mom did get a dryer in the basement. Then when we were grown up and did not need the small bedroom downstairs, my parents turned it into a laundry room with a washer and dryer on the main floor. This happened sometime in the later 1960s. That was so much easier for Mom and saved her from a lot of hard work! They did not do this sooner as my aunt Emma slept in that small room when she visited. Also, my mom took care of her dad, John Fischer, for many years and he used that small bedroom. I was thinking of all of Mom's work and how much easier we have it now when doing laundry! Thankfully, I hardly ever even need to get out the iron and ironing board to iron something.

Usually when hanging the laundry out in the backyard you could hear the bees buzzing around, birds singing, the chickens clucking contentedly in their fenced in area close by, and cows mooing in the pasture. It was a nice peaceful scene, but once and awhile we had some disturbances that we got used to. When working outside, there would be the rumblings of large guns being shot in the distance. There was a training base for servicemen at a place called Camp Claybanks sixteen and a half miles from our house. This was located along the bluffs of Lake Michigan and was opened in 1953 and closed in 1958. They could house 500 to 600 trainees at a time and the servicemen came from Michigan, Illinois, Iowa, and Indiana. The servicemen were taught how to shoot anti-aircraft missiles. There were positions for sixteen guns up to ninety-millimeters in size and could shoot ten miles out over the lake. A launch pad was built that would catapult remote controlled airplanes that were flown out over Lake Michigan. A variety of different range missiles were fired at the airplanes for practice, but at targets right behind the planes. The planes were expensive so they did not want them destroyed. I read on the internet that the shooting occurred between 7 a.m. and 7 p.m. and no boats were allowed in the area between those times. Sixteen and a half miles was quite a long distance away, but you still often heard the guns firing away sounding like the rumble of thunder!

Other very loud booming sounds we were accustomed to hearing in our area were the occasional sonic booms from jets breaking the sound barrier. This happened in the late 1950s and early 1960s in Oceana County (where we lived). There were military jet fighters practicing drills, and they often came from the west and headed east towards an air force base. They would exceed the speed of sound causing the sonic booms. They were very loud and sometimes could cause things to rattle in our cupboards. It often happened when you did not expect it, giving you quite a fright and disrupting our tranquility on the farm!

SUMMERS AND BUMBLEBEES, THE MILKMAN, CHRISTMAS TIME

We did not do a lot of really special things when growing up on the farm. Maybe the folks would take us, when we were younger, on a picnic twice a summer and swimming once or twice. Also, my younger sister and I were the youngest in our family thus our parents were getting older. It seems like we were always busy with farm work, yard work, and gardening; evenings my folks enjoyed resting and taking it easy. I cannot say we ever complained about it; that is just the way it was. There would be various picnics, reunions, get-togethers at the school, and it was always fun then to have a lot of kids to play with. I mentioned before how our cousins lived only half of a mile down the road from us, and we went back and forth a lot to play. We played outside most of the time. I think when our moms were so busy during the day, they did not want us underfoot.

Outdoors, we played croquet, kick the can, cowboys and Indians, Simon Says, hopscotch, baseball, jump rope, rode bikes, and eenie-I-over (throwing a ball over the roof). We also played in the barn a lot, in ours and in the cousins'. We liked making tunnels and playing in the stored bales of hay. Hide and seek was a favorite game. I remember getting in a little trouble one time. We were down at the cousins' place playing hide and seek. We decided a good place for Ron and Darlene to hide, the youngest two, was up on the small roof between the silo and barn. So I pushed them up to hide. It was not long before we heard very loud screaming and crying! The cousins' mom even heard them from in the house and hurried out to see what had happened. They both had gotten stung by bumblebees! Since they were up on the roof, they could not get away from the angry bees. We quickly helped the hurting and upset kids down.

We had a silo on our farm too, which was used to store silage. Silage was chopped up corn stalks for the cattle. Darlene and I, and the cousins, would climb up in our silo in the inside chute with a ladder. It was often filled with spider webs and spiders. But we would climb up through the spider webs to the open top of the silo. What fun to jump down from the top when it was about half full with silage. It was a wonder, though, that no one ever twisted their ankle or got hurt! I believe the silo was about thirty feet tall.

For the times we did play inside and often on Sunday afternoons, we had multiple games we would play: checkers, dominoes, carrom, Rummy Royal, Dirty Twos, Bingo, jacks, Frustration, Old Maid, Sorry, Hide the Thimble, and Who's Got the Button. For that game, several would sit on the stairsteps. The one who held the button would stand on the steps backwards facing the sitting kids. That person would hide the button in a hand and hold both hands closed, and top of the hands up to one person at a time. The person who guessed the correct hand could then move down a step. The one who made it down the stairs first was the person to hide the button in their hands the next time. Another thing we had great fun doing was shutting all the lights off in the house evenings and try to find someone. We did this when the parents were away. Our folks did not like us doing this as they were afraid we would knock something over and break it. We also had a small record player that played the small-sized, 45 speed records. We liked to act out the stories on the record called "Peter and the Wolf" and "The Little White Duck." We played we were the animals, climbed the furniture for our trees, and acted along as the story was sung.

My dad raised milk cows from six at a time, to as many as twenty cows. He really liked his cows and treated them well; of course, they were all like pets and had names. So we always had plenty of milk in our refrigerator. You could not get fresher milk as a pail full would be brought in from the morning milking, strained, and then used on our cereal for breakfast. We loved it while still warm from the cows.

Dad tried to make some money selling the milk. At first, all the cows were milked by hand. Dad and brother Herb were responsible for the morning and evening milking when I was a youngster. All the barn cats knew when it was milking time too and would sit lined up for fresh milk. The clever cats were skilled at catching the milk when Dad or Herb would squirt the milk in the air towards their mouths. It was fun watching these talented cats with their trick. They always got more milk in their bowls too, after the milking was completed. Hand milking was done on a three-legged stool often with your head and shoulder leaning on the cow. I remember one time Herb got head lice and Mom thought maybe from leaning on a cow while milking it, but more likely he caught the lice elsewhere.

When they milked their pails full, the milk was dumped into the milk cans, maybe two or three of them. They were metal cans about two and a half feet tall. Those cans were then stored in a tank of cold water until the milkman came in a truck to pick them up. I do not know if Darlene and I could hear the truck coming or how we knew when he would arrive, but we always would quickly hide in exactly the same place in the barn. When the milkman (we remember his name being Mr. Moon) came in the barn to pick up the cans of milk, we would jump out and holler "*BOO.*" He would always act very, very scared! We would do this over and over again throughout the week when we were little. Later, when my brother Herb was in high school and played football, we got a milking machine to help with our work. Dad was working the second shift in Muskegon, so Herb had to do the evening milking. During football season, when Herb had to stay after school for practice, Mom and I would have to start the milking. Herb would finish it up when he got home. They even ran a bus to bring the kids home from football practice.

Christmas was a wonderful and special time. One thing I always remember is the decorated outdoor pine tree. The tradition got started when the tree was small, maybe five or six feet tall. But as the tree kept growing, so did the amount of strings of lights needed to decorate it. Soon it was so tall that Dad and Herb would use the tractor with a bucket and put the bucket as tall as they could. My brother would stand in the bucket to decorate the tree. Finally, it got so tall that he would just climb up the middle of the pine by the trunk to decorate the very top. You could see that beautiful lighted tree for miles around!

It was so exciting when Christmas rolled around, and I looked so forward to it. The whole extended family would come and we would have a wonderful Christmas dinner. The rule was the dishes always had to be done before we could open any presents. Somehow, Mom had a Santa Claus suit stored in the attic. She would persuade her older son or son-in-law to put it on and surprise us, when we were little, with an appearance from Santa. I remember when Darlene was about two and I was about six, we received our one and only doll. We were so excited and happy with them. We did not get as many presents as kids often do today, but we were very happy with the presents we eagerly opened. It often was new pajamas or new clothes and not so many toys. I will never forget the present I got from Darlene when she was little. She had thought up the idea of this present and wrapped it up; I do not know if my mom knew or not. When I opened it up, it was a small box full of colored shavings from sharpened crayons. I honestly think she thought they were so pretty and that I would like them for a present! I do not think I did, but I had to act surprised. One other unusual gift Herb, Darlene, and I would often receive from our aunt Emma was a whole large bag of potato chips. We just thought that was the best thing to have our very own bag of chips all to ourselves. She probably included a little money with it too.

Those family get-togethers meant so much to me when growing up. It was a lot of fun to have brothers, sisters, spouses, nieces and nephews all around on Christmas day and for other special happenings. There was always a lot of laughter, good fellowship, good food, and great times. I think that is why to this day it means so much to me now with my own family, and to have everyone around for special occasions. Some of our family live in Michigan, some in Texas, and some in South Dakota; the best thing is always to have all my family home all together. I always tell my family, "I like to have all your feet under my kitchen table" for special holidays and special events. I am sure most families feel this way also. Can anything compare with the joy, delight, and pleasure of occasions spent with the whole family? These times to visit, times to play together, work together, times when we are serious and need comforting, and times to bond together are invaluable in making wonderful and lasting memories. I think at an early age, we may not appreciate these things as much as we should. When we get older, we get a little wiser and more perceptive about treasuring and valuing significant and meaningful things.

A BROKEN LEG, CREATIVE PLAY, SHOCKED

I had to get my brother Herb's memories for this next story, because he was the recipient of this accident (and I was only a baby). My older sister, Elinor, has already passed away, so I could not ask her. We had not moved out to the farm yet, but we were working out there planting and harvesting some crops while still living in Muskegon. Herb said he was about four when it happened. Dad had borrowed Uncle Henry's Ford tractor and Elinor was driving it for the first time. They were pulling a wagon while brother Don and Dad were loading corn stalks that later would be chopped and put in the silo. Herb was on the tractor standing on the foot rest on the left side by the clutch. He was holding on to the steering wheel, when Elinor turned it and jerked the tractor. Herb fell backwards and was run over by the back wheel. His left leg was broken which was odd as it would have seemed like his right leg would have been hit first. It scared Elinor so, and she felt so terribly bad that she never drove a farm tractor after that! I am sure they were all very, very thankful Herb only wound up with a broken leg and not something much more serious!

Soon after the broken leg event, Herb remembers while he was recovering in bed with his broken leg, Dad had to do some work above in the attic that had no flooring. He had to cross on the floor joists and somehow slipped, and his legs came through the ceiling—one foot hanging down in Herb's room and the other foot in another room. Fortunately, he straddled the wall and did not come down on Herb in the bed . . . just a lot of ceiling plaster came down! My mom often told this story as she found it hilarious; she said she just laughed and laughed as it was so funny to see the legs coming through the ceiling. I am sure Dad would not have shared in her hearty laughter as that would have meant another thing for him to fix and a terrible mess to clean up!

It seems when living on the farm, we were more creative in what we came up with to play. After a heavy rain, we liked going out with rubber boots and playing in the puddles. Or, when the rains filled the ditch in front of our house and barn, what fun to build our own little boats and sail them down the ditches. Dad always had scraps of wood we could use in the garage. Also, we had clip-on roller skates to fasten on our shoes, which never worked all that great being they slipped back off easily. Since the driveway was not paved then, we would skate in the basement on the cement floor and go around and around the furnace, which was in the middle of the basement. This was not a huge area, but we made it work and had fun.

As we got older, we liked to climb trees and we had our favorites. To the west of the house there were three old apple trees. They never had any usable apples as they were too small and full of worms, but those trees were the best for climbing. The branches just seemed to be in the right places for climbing quite high. We were never told not to do this, and I guess we were careful enough as we never fell out of the trees either. Another thing we played in was the large corncrib that was used for storing the husked ears of corn. When it was empty, before the corn was harvested, what a nice place to play "house." My brother Herb said that this corncrib was made from the red pines from our 80 acres up the road. The flooring came from our schoolhouse after there was a fire.

Once in awhile we played in the woods bordering our property to the east. We had it in our minds to make a log cabin and we were using trunks of smaller trees that had fallen down in the woods. We only got it about two feet high and then lost interest and forgot about it. I was wondering when I fell asleep last night if there would be any evidence of it. I would like to check it out but I think it would be too overgrown to try and find it. Oddly enough, I had a couple of dreams about being in that same spot in the woods. In my dreams we had a really big and nice tree house with a fire pit and a swing nearby. Dreams are funny—how that comes back in the subconscious mind some sixty-five and more years later.

We always seemed to come up with resourceful and good imaginative play. It makes you wonder if children today are missing out on the opportunity to be creative and imaginative. When they can so easily turn on the television, play all their hand held games, are on cell phones so much and computers, are all these electronic devices taking the place of inventive and productive creative play? Do parents watch and monitor this enough and encourage their children to get outside and ride bikes, play sports, and get exercise? Do kids still get together to play ball, hide and seek, kick the can, and other fun things? Or are some of these things just all in the past? I hope not.

Continuing on, I had a shocking occurrence happen when I was eight or nine years old and trying to learn to ride a bicycle all by myself. It was a regular-sized two-wheeler as we did not have any middle-sized bikes back then. I would get on and start up by the house and go down the slight hill on the dirt driveway towards the barn. This one time, somehow, I was off balance and could not keep it on the driveway and went down a little hill by the lower part of the barn. The bad thing was, I could not stop and went right into the electric fence that kept the cows in the barnyard. I was caught in it and could not get loose! All the while . . . zap, zap, zap, zap . . . as the current went through the fence and me! At least Darlene was outside, and I hollered for her to get Mom since Dad was gone some place. It took a while for Darlene to do this and so more zap, zap, zap which did not feel good at all! It was not a terribly strong current but enough to get quite a jolt. Mom came hurriedly down when she saw what was going on, quickly got the current shut off in the barn, and got me loose. I remember I did not feel very good the rest of the afternoon! I went to bed to rest, and when Dad came home he came to see how I was feeling. I did learn to ride bike eventually and did not end up in the electric fence again!

I was not the only one that got shocked on that fence, besides the cows, that is. They learned about electric fences quite quickly. Once or twice of being shocked, and the cows would remember to not go too near it again. My young niece got shocked once also. Darlene remembers this happening when my older sister, her husband, and their two girls stayed with us awhile. They took care of us while our folks took a trip to North Dakota to see relatives. My niece, of maybe six to eight years, was told by her dad not to touch the fence. One day, she must have wanted to test it and grabbed hold of the fence with both hands. Sharon really got shocked because she was standing in wet grass, and so she could not get loose. Darlene remembers she finally got her pulled off. It may not sound the best to have had an electric fence, but it was a lot easier to put up. You usually only needed one strand of wire connected to the fence poles. The other fences we had were with posts cut from trees with two or three strands of barbed wire. The hardest work for installing those fences was digging the holes for the posts, or sometimes making the posts. I remember helping dig the post holes sometimes when older. We also pastured our cows part of the year on the 80 acres and used the barbed wire fences since there was no electricity on that piece of property. Maybe some of these fences seemed a bit extreme with the electric current or the barbed wires, but they were needed to keep the cows from getting out of the pastures.

If they got out, they would eat vegetables in the garden, corn in fields, or ruin the plantings or crops in neighboring fields. You did not want neighbors getting angry with you, so you did your best to keep the cattle in the fences!

CARTWRIGHT SCHOOL, LOST TEETH, WINTERS

As youngsters, we attended a one-room schoolhouse, Cartwright School, that was one mile from our farm. I do not have the date when this school was started, but either in the late 1800s or early 1900s. I say this, since in a county history book my dad's brothers and sisters were listed as attending in 1905. My dad was born in 1903 so would have started there about 1908. The land for the school was first purchased from Jacob Van Dyke. But, a Clarence Cartwright attended the school, so that must be where the name came from. My brother, Herb, remembers a coal and wood furnace in the front southeast corner of the school. Also, there were two outhouses out back. The teacher had to get the furnace going each morning, or sometimes, one of the close neighbors to the school would build the fire, warming the school. An addition was added to the back of the school by the time I started in 1948. I never had to use the outhouses since the addition included a furnace, a small kitchen, and a girls' and boys' bathroom.

My mom also attended a one-room schoolhouse called Batten School that was built in 1904. It was located a little over two miles from Cartwright School. In the history book about Oceana

County, it stated that sometimes teachers boarded with a family in the neighborhood during the week. Teachers back then were qualified for teaching by attending County Normal for one year after high school. An average pay could be from $35 to $75 per month depending on how many pupils were attending. The teachers had to teach all the grades from kindergarten through eighth grade. Gradually these one-room schools were closed, consolidated with other schools, and the pupils transported by bus to schools farther away. Cartwright School was open until the 1960s, then was bought by an individual and used as a hunting lodge until either 2018 or 2019. I was surprised to drive by and see my old country school is now gone.

Every day and often in rain or in snowstorms, we would make that mile trek over the dirt road to the school. When I was little, I must have walked with Herb, though I do not remember this. Two years later my cousin Betty started school, so I walked with her. A couple years after that my sister, Darlene, and Betty's younger brother joined us, as well as the Zuders who lived on the corner near us. And of course, we had to walk back home also. Once and awhile, we would cut through the fields to make this trip a bit shorter. Some days, to pass the time while walking, we would try to kick a stone all the way there. Often we would sing songs we learned at school or Sunday School choruses most of the way there or back. Occasionally, if it was pouring rain, either my mom or my cousins' mom would come with the car to give us a ride home. When we were older, we would ride our bikes most of the time when the weather was favorable. My bike was just a made up bike of an old frame and various parts Dad found in the garage, and I had painted it black and silver. It did not even have regular handlebars but some piping my dad used. He just cut pieces of rubber that fit on for the handle grips. It worked all right and transported me where I needed to go.

Our desks at school were the sturdy wooden ones with tops that opened and underneath you stored your books, papers, crayons, and pencils. I recall how one day when I was probably in the 6th or 7th grade, I began feeling a little warm and uncomfortable. Measles, or maybe it was the chickenpox, were going around and I was aware of this. I went to the bathroom and looked in the mirror and sure enough . . . I saw a few red spots appearing on my face. For some reason (probably because I was shy), I did not want to tell the teacher and draw attention to myself. I crept back to my seat with my head lowered, and quietly sat down. It was not very long before we would be dismissed to go home, maybe half an hour to an hour. So that whole time, I hid my face behind my opened desk top and pretended to be cleaning the inside of my desk and kept rearranging it until it was time to go home. Then I could quickly sneak out, grab my jacket and lunch pail before anyone noticed my red spots, and make my way home (and I would have been confined at home for a week to ten days). You always caught the childhood diseases as they went around. I remember getting the mumps twice though they say you can only get them once. Maybe I got them on one side first then the other.

The teachers we had seemed well organized for the most part and able to teach and keep the children in control. The average attendance was about eighteen pupils, sometimes more and sometimes less. Throughout the day, each grade would go up and sit in chairs by the teacher's desk to quietly read to her, recite something, or be quizzed on their lessons. The remaining students during this time would work quietly at their desks on penmanship, reading, math, or other subjects. Somehow, these one room schoolhouses worked, and we liked going there. The big excitement always was Christmas time and the programs we would perform for our parents and the rest of our families. We would be so thrilled and nervous about saying our parts, being in a play, and singing songs. There would be a stage set up with a curtain. For the program, we would loudly and with gusto sing "Up On the House Top," "Here Comes Santa Claus," "Frosty The Snowman," "Silent Night," "Away in the Manger," "We

Three Kings," and "Deck the Halls" to list a few. Sometimes, there would be an opportunity to play a piano solo or a different instrument. I know I once played "Silent Night" on an autoharp my mom had bought. It was not much of a solo in that I just plucked one string at a time, since I did not know how to strum it. I quickly did just one verse as I was pretty shy about doing it. We always looked forward to the treat after the program which almost always was a paper bag full of small hard candies, along with an orange or an apple.

I do not remember the year, but the very afternoon before the Christmas play there was a fire in the school. The fire burned most of the south end of the school, going through the roof. All the families had to be contacted that there would be no Christmas play in the evening or school until further notice. We had a nice long Christmas break that year! Part of the roof had to be replaced and most of the inside on that end of the school. They did not find the cause of the fire. The parents did a lot of the repair work, and we did not have to go back to school for weeks. After we did go back, the encyclopedias and books in the back always smelled like smoke.

There were two teachers many of us really liked and were our favorites: Mrs. Mary Bartlett and Mrs. Kelly Hansen. I will say Mrs. Hansen was still one of my favorites, although the only time I ever had to stay after school was when she dished out the punishment. After our two recesses and our lunch time, the teacher pulled a rope connected to the bell in the back coatroom, signaling that it was time to come back in. This one time when I was about a 7th grader, I told some other kids to help hold the doors shut. There were two doors to this back entrance, so we held each door shut so the teacher could not come out to ring the bell. We thought it was a funny little joke, and we did not hold the doors very long. But Mrs. Hansen did not appreciate this joke and made the four of us stay after school for probably a half hour. I remember the mother of my sister's friend had come to school for some reason, and she just laughed and laughed at our plight.

Recess and lunch times at school were always fun. We usually played outside and played a variety of games. We often played baseball, kick the can, steal sticks, and eenie-I-over. During winters it was sliding, Fox and Geese, snow forts, building snowmen together, and good old snowball fights. But of course, it was not always playing in harmony, and occasionally, a fight would break out among the older boys. One older kid happened to have a temper problem. One day he got mad and really pounded a younger kid causing him to have a bloody nose, bloody mouth, and a tooth knocked out. There was no "911" in those days, so the teacher would have to take care of any injuries. If anything too bad happened, there was a house crossways from the school where someone could use a phone.

I recall one serious accident, and I think the mother was called to come to school to get her son. Larry was in my grade, and it happened when we were in about the 6th grade. During recess in the winters, we were allowed to go across the road to a nice sliding hill on the road kitty-corner from the school. Most of the children had sleds with runners, and they would sail down the hill at a pretty good speed. Sometimes, we would cross the other road, or if a car was coming turned into a field. Neither of the roads had much traffic. Other times, we would turn into the neighbor's back driveway. This one time, Larry was going too fast to make the turn in the driveway and instead started going under a building that sat up on blocks. He was riding the sled on his stomach and hit his mouth on the bottom of the building and knocked a tooth out. That sure must have hurt!

I liked school and did well in my subjects. I really liked spelling, and it was fun when we had spelling bees. In younger grades, we would practice penmanship, and I would practice and practice to try and get it so perfect. We would print or write on those papers with wide and dotted lines. It seems like we had quite a bit of free time after our lessons were completed. We could do what we wanted then as long as we sat quietly at our desks. Some kids would read, some drew pictures, and I liked using the old encyclopedias and looked up about horses in order to draw them. One of the best things for me about grade school was playing baseball, and we played it a lot during recesses and lunch hour! In the spring, the kids in the older grades would be on a team, and we would compete with different local schools. This was an all boys' team but since our school did not have many students, it was short on players. I was happy and excited to be asked to play on the team. I could not throw very far so my position was short stop between second and third bases. Some of the pitchers could pitch pretty fast, and I felt rather bad when I almost always struck out. I have thoroughly enjoyed sports all my life probably because of playing baseball and all the outdoor games when I was younger.

We only had three students in the class when I graduated from eighth grade, so we combined our graduation ceremony with another country school, also only having three graduating. So next, a summer break and soon it would be off to high school for me. I liked our little country school and did not like to think about riding a bus to the high school fourteen miles away. In fact, weeks before it was time for me to start attending Montague High School, I really got worried and panicked. I worried and worried and sometimes cried myself to sleep nights as I did not want to go to that big high school of four hundred students! I was used to a small school with only eighteen students! I remember my mom coming upstairs to my room a night or two to try and console me and give me encouragement. I could at least get to sleep then, but I still was pretty apprehensive my first day and for the first few weeks of high school. My brother was a senior then, but he was not much help as he had his own friends. After awhile, I got used to the routine, made new friends, and high school was not bad at all.

When our winters came bustling in, we could have some big and wild storms back then. You went to school, though, no matter how big the storm or how much snow you had to wade through.

Schools were rarely canceled! The snow plows they had were not the large plows with the long extended blades that can push the snow way back from the roads like we have today. Nor did they have the huge snow blower equipment. Instead, the banks would get higher and higher. When we would be walking on the road to or from school, and if we heard a snowplow coming, we would have to scramble like mad to get up on the snow banks out of the way. In some places where the snow accumulation was greater, there were times we would be standing on snow banks much higher than the snowplows!

My sister, Darlene, reminded me of the time when our cousin, Ron, convinced us to take a shortcut across our fields one winter day on our way home from school. There was often a wet spot in a field on the back of our property, and Darlene mistakenly went through the ice and got her feet wet. By the time we arrived home, she was so cold her teeth were chattering. Mom wanted to make sure she was not ill so proceeded to take her temperature. Darlene said her teeth were chattering so bad she actually broke the thermometer.

Another winter day, we had a really bad ice storm that left a layer of ice on all the roads and fields. We walked to school in the morning, but my mom came to pick us up with the car in the afternoon. That was a mistake because she could not make it back up the hills. She had to go way around on a different road and barely made it home on that route, since there also were some big hills. But boy did we have fun playing when we got home! Our sleds would stay right on top of that crust of ice, and we would ride and ride right across the fields—even on hills that were very small. We could keep on sliding and sailing smoothly forever . . . what fun! As I tell about this, I can still envision that day when we were cruising, soaring, and gliding across those fields on our sleds with the cool breeze in our faces. Those icy conditions did not happen very often, and were just perfect for all that extraordinary enjoyment on that day!

MULBERRIES, FIRE TOWER, STUMPS

I mentioned, previously, that one of my mom's baked goods specialties was her very delicious pies. Added to that list of various pies was one of my favorites, mulberry pie. We had a very large mulberry tree located on the west edge of our property. I do not know if early ancestors planted it or if it came up on its own. There are several colors of mulberries; ours were the deep dark blue or purple variety. I found it interesting, when looking up about mulberries, that they are grown in Asia and North America, and their leaves are the only food that silkworms eat. Unlike a lot of berries with a short producing season, mulberries are ripe over an extended period, several months, from mid to late summer. Darlene, my two cousins, and I always felt it a very important duty and obligation each summer to pick mulberries so my mom could make a pie or two. The cousins would bring their containers of berries home to their family. We never wanted to miss out on this. It was quite an undertaking, and it could take at least half a day to accomplish our very important berry picking task. First, we would drag our six to eight foot heavy wooden stepladder, pull our wagon with lots of buckets and containers, and make our journey across the fields to our destination. We would pick and pick to fill our buckets, visit, have a good time and wind up with very purple fingers! Next, we would drag all the stuff back across the fields home and wait for the reward of that mouth-watering, tasty pie. So, it was quite a procedure but well worth the effort! Another pie my mom would sometimes make was elderberry. These were very, very tiny berries that grew in a big cluster. Since the berries were so tiny, you needed to pick a lot to have enough for one pie. We would find them in the ditches along our swamp. I would help Mom pick the buckets full, but I did not care for this pie at all. Even though my mom added a lot of sugar, it still tasted sour to me!

Besides the mulberry picking escapade, we had another adventure in our area to participate in almost a mile away. We often rode our bikes or walked to the Ferry Fire Tower, about a hundred-foot high wooden structure with a small room on top. Sometimes, we just went there for something to do but did not climb it. Other times we would climb it, but I did not do it very often as it was too high! The lower steps going up were okay and had a flat railing to hold on to, but the very last dozen steps into the top room were straight up on a ladder, which was so scary! There were often wasps under the railings that we had to watch out for or we would get stung! We climbed this one time on a field trip when in grade school. The lady manning the tower explained what all the machines were for and what she had to do when she spotted smoke. If anything looked suspicious, she would call and notify the proper personnel about the possible fire. That was quite the unusual job to climb that high tower every day, except she would not have to when raining or during the winter. The lady who did this for many, many years was a neighbor lady to the west about a mile. I sure do not know how she ever got that job. I read that these fire towers gained in popularity around 1910. Also, it stated on the internet that in 1933, during the Great Depression, President Franklin Roosevelt formed the Civilian Conservation Corps (CCC). It consisted of young men and veterans of World

War I. It was during this time that the CCC built a lot of lookout towers, so perhaps that is when the Ferry Fire Tower also came into existence. I should have asked my dad years ago when it was built and by whom. When planes and more modern technology took over the role of the manned fire towers, the bottom two tiers of steps were removed to discourage kids from climbing the tower and maybe getting hurt. Kids still managed to climb it though, my husband being one of them. Beyond the fire tower on a little two-track road, we would like to look for arbutus flowers (also called the mayflower). They came out in early spring: a very small white and pink flower that grew close to the ground and they had the sweetest smell!

I must not have been too greatly frightened about heights. Darlene, the cousins, and I would cross the large wooden beams in our barn which were very high! It would not have been good if we would have slipped and fallen with the hard, cement floor below us! Dad would have gotten after us if he had known we were doing this. Another thing we did in the barn, which was so much fun, was swing on the bag swing. My dad and brother made this, the heavy rope being tied way up in the rafters. You sat and swung on this grain bag, chucked full of straw. You had to climb a ladder up to the loft, which was about eight to ten feet tall. From there, you could jump on the bag swing and swing way, way out over the barn floor. Again, the cement floor was under us, but we never fell off.

We also had a basketball hoop in the barn where we could shoot baskets. My brother, Herb, liked to play basketball with his friends and would play some evenings. They often played in a friend's barn as their set up was nicer; it had a larger area to play and a better cement floor. Our barn flooring was rough and cracked in spots. One evening when playing basketball with his friends, Herb had the misfortune of bumping into the wall, and the only thing hitting the wall was his tooth. Nothing else on his face got hurt, but he chipped his tooth badly. He did not dare tell our parents when he came home that evening. The next morning, when he was eating breakfast, my mom said something that made Herb laugh. Then she saw it—that part of his front tooth was missing, so a trip to the dentist was needed. The tooth was pulled as it was split way up into the root. The way they fixed it back then was with a false tooth that was fastened to a plate that fit in the roof of his mouth. He usually took it out when he went to bed and when he played sports. One time when Herb was swimming with friends in a lake close by, it came out in the dark and no one could find it. He went back the next morning and actually still found it! After getting that false tooth, Herb always had lots of fun surprising people, especially the girls, and would smile and drop his tooth. He could use his tongue and get that plate to come down which looked very funny! He relates the fun he had with some of the girls in a study hall at school. He would hide the tooth in his mouth and when he smiled, they would think he had a missing tooth. When a girl tapped someone else to show her, he would smile again with it in place. He had this for a long time, even as an adult, but then his dentist finally talked him into getting a permanent tooth.

Another thing that was different, that we thought was a lot of fun, was playing on the stumps. Across the road from our barn was a row of large stumps along the side of the road with a ditch in between. Whoever owned that property years ago, rather than burning all those stumps, just dragged them to the edge of the field there. There were a lot of them, but they were in a nice straight line and all close together forming a row. Maybe they should have been called a root fence as lots of roots were left all over the stumps. They were all weathered and quite smooth from being out in the elements for years and years. Roots were branching out in all different directions: high ones, low ones, and ones going sideways. We had so much fun climbing from one end of the stump and root row to the other end, and doing it over and over again. It was quite a long row! I mentioned earlier that we did not have a lot of toys, but it did not matter. There were so many other things to do and play on the farm that we were not bored. We had a lot of creative and imaginative things to play, and we played outdoors a lot! It helped, too, that the cousins lived so close, so we had friends to play with. We could just walk back and forth the half mile so our moms did not have to drive us. Roy Rogers and Gene Autry were popular at that time on the TV shows, so we often played cowboys and Indians. I liked Roy Rogers the best so always played I was Roy Rogers, and Darlene was Gene Autry. I do not remember who my cousins played, but I emailed Betty and she thought maybe the Cisco Kid for one, or the Lone Ranger. When playing Indians, I was always Red Feather and Darlene, Blue Feather. It seems like we could have come up with more original names.

One warm summer day, some of us decided to take a bike ride to a little lake (called Bear Lake) two roads to the north of us. This was riding on all gravel roads as none of them were paved back then. We did this and somehow decided to take a longer ride into New Era. It was rather silly of us since it was a very hot day; we never carried any water with us, and our parents would not have known about that decision. Plus, the road we decided to take (we thought it would be a short cut) was a two-track about three fourths of the way. Most of this two-track consisted of very loose, fine sand so we wound up pushing our bikes more than we rode them. By the time we made it to New Era, five miles away, we were dying of thirst. We rode over to my sister-in-law's house, and she gave us water. We were so thirsty that water never tasted so good! I think we called home to our moms to let them know where we were. This was just a spur of the moment decision that turned out to be a hot time and a bit tiring.

Those were good times growing up, and I look back with fondness when thinking about our various activities. Our parents were always there for us, and we felt their love and support; we had friends to do things with. There was not so much of the continuous chasing around like families have to do today, and you spent a lot of time at home with neighbors, family, and friends. And to me, that was good! It was a peaceful, orderly, tranquil place where we could be content in the environment we grew up in. I was fond of the farm and enjoyed the country life!

HOEING, BY THE CREEK, ASPARAGUS

Growing up on the farm meant you learned how to work too, which is okay. I think it is a real asset that children at a young age are taught how to work. Nowadays, many children do not have that opportunity to find jobs at a young age which teaches them how to be responsible, dependable, and teaches the value of earning and saving money. We had many such opportunities for work, and I think it was good for us. When our four daughters were growing up, they too had opportunities to find work during the summers learning invaluable lessons. They are all good workers as grown-ups and know how to give an employer a good day's work.

On a typical sunny summer day our farm family was usually outdoors playing or working. There was the yard work that needed to be done, a sizable lawn that had to be mowed, and my folks planted a very large garden. That meant there was almost constantly weeding and hoeing to be done in the garden when we were not busy doing something else. We always had a big supply of fresh vegetables from our garden. Some of the early things harvested were peas and radishes. Dad liked radish sandwiches which I did not care for! The sandwiches just had lots of butter spread on the bread with the sliced radishes and maybe some added salt. Something Darlene and I did like, though, was Mom occasionally fixed heated kidney beans with added vinegar and bacon. It was a very tasty combination and something I still fix once and awhile (Darlene said she does too).

We were young children when we were expected to help out with the work. During the summers, a favorite thing to do was to run around barefoot. On this one certain hot summer day, that was a big mistake! My dad grabbed my brother and me to help him hoe some beans on our 80 acres. This was a large field to hoe by hand, and it was a very hot, sunny day! I soon found out when hoeing that the sand was terribly hot, and I had not thought to grab any shoes. Here I was hurrying from bean plant to bean plant trying to stand in the plant's very tiny spot of shade while hoeing. This was not a very fun experience! I did not remember what Dad raised the beans for, and recently asked my brother Herb. He said they were dry beans, and Dad would raise either red or navy beans. When they were ready, they were pulled and stacked in or by the barn. Then a neighbor who had a tractor and a thresher would come and separate the beans, the fodder going in the barn for bedding for animals and the beans in sacks. For years there was a device that would drop the beans slowly on a belt that a person would run with a foot peddle and sort the beans by hand. The good beans went into sacks and then were sold to the feed mill. I remember this machine sitting in the kitchen sometimes where anyone who had time could sit and sort. Other times, it sat in the shed connected to the house. I did this sometimes too, picking little stones out of the beans. Mom would keep her share of beans also for soups. My older brother, Don, planted yellow beans for a cash crop also. He had to get everyone he could to help pick them, and they were sold to the canning company five miles away. My mom was a very fast picker; either Darlene or I would keep busy just bringing her empty baskets and emptying the full ones.

Another cash crop that Dad tried for a year or so was raising potatoes. My mom's brother had a tractor-pulled digger that farmers borrowed, or he came and dug the potatoes. I remember a field in the back corner of our property one year and the rows and rows of potatoes that we needed to pick up. Herb said that in the forties and fifties this was a popular cash crop, and sometimes those who raised the potatoes had to keep their kids out of school just to get the potatoes picked up. Thinking back, picking up the potatoes was not as bad as loading up stones. That was a job I really did not like! We would take the tractor and trailer and make round after round on a worked up field picking up the stones that had appeared. You had to walk several yards beyond the trailer and carry the stones back, and some could be quite heavy. This was not a small trailer, but more the size of a smaller farm wagon, so we could pile on a large load of stones and rocks. We had a place to dump the rocks on the 80 and a closer place on the back of our farm. It would often be wet by the rock pile on the farm, so we would frequently see snakes in that area.

Just a little explanation about the 80 acres of land we owned one mile up the road and west from our farm. It was a beautiful piece of land! There was a section of red pines in the northwest corner that was probably about Christmas tree size when we moved to the farm. They possibly were planted in the 1930s when the government had a program for planting red pines. They were beautiful trees (still are), and Dad spent a lot of time trimming all the lower branches off over the years. He planted another field of pine trees on the 80, when first purchasing that land, that we used for Christmas trees until they got too big. A creek also runs through part of this property. I know my dad always thought it would have been nice to build a home on the hill overlooking the creek in his later years, but that never happened. There were six fields that were cleared for growing crops. One of the larger cleared fields on the west side of the 80 still had stumps on it when Dad bought the property. Dad had someone with a bulldozer come and push them in a big pile that they burned. Before that, my brother Herb stated that they would hook a team of horses to a long pole that was fastened to the stump with a chain. Then, they would drive the horses in a circle around the stump until it was twisted out of the ground. Sometimes they made stump fences with those removed stumps.

I recall an unusual story involving the tractor and trailer when we were heading to that 80 one day. It may have been to pick up stones or maybe to pick up some hay bales. I think either Herb or Don was driving. My sister and I (and maybe our cousins) were riding on the empty trailer. We were used to riding on the trailer often so were standing up and were very adept at standing. For some reason, we got the idea of jumping on the back of the trailer, which would make it bounce up and down. This is because a trailer only has two wheels in the middle and is not like a hay wagon with four wheels. We were doing the jumping for fun, and we would go higher with our jumping when we hit bumps. But alas, all that jumping made the hitch pin wiggle loose on the hitch and what a big surprise to us—the trailer came unhooked! We kept rolling on the unhooked trailer, and it swerved heading down the big ditch. This was a very steep side hill by the creek on our 80 acres. We all thought the trailer with its worried and frightened riders were going to wind up in the creek! The creek was wide and deep there since it never went though the culvert right, and it was all backed up. Halfway down the steep grade a small fence stopped us, but our driver was not at all happy about our quandary. I do not remember how we got the big, heavy trailer back up. Maybe we had a rope or chain along and pulled it up with the tractor. At least no one was hurt, but it could have been much worse if we all would have wound up in the creek!

Loading wood, after Dad had cut it up, was a job we were expected to help with. In our early days, we still had a furnace in the basement that burned wood or coal. Dad often cut up wood on the 80 or on the home farm with a huge saw run by a long belt connected to the pulley on our tractor. We kids would have to load the wood on the trailer or in the back of the pick-up truck to be transported to the house. There, we had to unload it and throw it down a chute to the basement where Dad would stack it in the room where it was stored.

Sometimes, since coal was longer lasting and produced a more even heat, Dad would get a load from my mom's brother who owned a coal company. Fischer Coal Company was located in Muskegon, thirty miles away and was one of the major coal companies in the area. My uncle and aunt lived very close to the train tracks! Uncle Carl would get loads of coal by train and stored it in the many bins by his place. He distributed the coal by truck to businesses and home owners. There was something special about the wood and coal heat that made our house so toasty warm and cozy in the winters. It was so nice coming in from the cold and standing by a register to get warmed up. We often put our mittens and boots in front of the kitchen register to get them dry and warm. When Mom made homemade bread or rolls, the dough was set in front of the register to rise more quickly. And homemade noodles, too, were hung over the back of a chair on a clean cloth to dry in front of the kitchen register. Years later, when I drove a school bus as an adult, there was a family that heated with wood, and I could smell the smoke on their clothing when they boarded the bus. I liked the smell, which brought back good memories of when we grew up in the farmhouse heated with wood and coal.

Harvesting the field corn was another job that had to be done. I was not school age yet when they used to cut the cornstalks off at ground level and put them in shocks to dry. Then either they picked the corn off in the field or brought the shocks to the barn to pick and used the stalks for bedding. When I was in grade school, we sometimes helped Dad pick the ears of corn off the stalks while they were still standing in rows in the cornfield. That was a slow process when picking the whole field by hand. Dad would keep at it faithfully for days and days and weeks until the job was completed. We would husk the ears, too, before tossing it on the trailer. Later years, he either hired a neighbor with a corn picker or borrowed a picker to harvest the corn. That went much faster even though all those first machines were only one row pickers. The picker would strip the ears off the stalk, next the ears would go through rotating rollers to remove the husks, and then go up the elevator belt to fall in the wagon pulled behind the picker. Today, they have very large corn pickers; some can do as many as sixteen corn rows at once!

During my earliest years, we had that huge threshing machine come to thresh the grain. Years after that, we would hire someone with a combine machine to harvest the grain in the fields. There was a hopper on the machine that the grain went into. Every few rounds it would have to be emptied into bags. Dad would be there with the tractor and trailer, or pick-up truck, to load up the bags. Once the bags were transported home, they had to be pulled up to the top of the garage where the grain was stored. Until we got older, Darlene and I together would pull the bags up with a rope and pulley.

Sometimes, Herb was around to pull the bags up. Dad would be upstairs in the garage to dump the bags of grain. There were four large bins up there so we could store the wheat, oats, rye, or other grains. The farm cats would get pretty plump when they tried to keep the mouse population down, as mice often found their way into the bins. It was difficult for us kids to get upstairs by the bins. We had to climb about six wooden slats nailed to a wall straight up, and the slats were far apart. But we would manage to go up there sometimes to play. When the bins had grain in them, there was such a nice fresh, yeasty smell.

All these farm jobs you just did with no complaining. You were part of the family and needed to help get things done. Then as we got older, we worked at my uncle Henry and aunt Dorothy's (Fischer) for pay. My first job there was picking asparagus. I was pretty young when I started, maybe in 5th grade. I remember that first time they put me on a row and told me what to do. It was an older patch but still produced a lot of asparagus with very, very wide rows! For my first time, they were even still using knives to cut the asparagus off rather than just snapping it off. I remember I was on my knees and looked down that row that was about two feet wide, and it looked so thick, like a miniature forest of trees. I thought that row would never end! I worked and worked but seemed to make little progress. It took so long cutting each piece with a knife. I do not think I ever finished that row, nor did they ask me to help much that first year.

After that, the method of harvesting asparagus turned to just snapping it off where it would snap naturally. That way you got the most tender part of the spears. Fischers eventually had four fields of asparagus and hired Darlene and me, along with my cousins, Betty and Ron to help. Between Uncle Henry and his two boys, and the four of us, we could keep up with the four fields. This was usually picked every other day but not on Sundays. Some days when it was very hot, it had to be picked two days or more in a row. It took us about four or five hours to pick all four fields.

An odd little incident happened one day with cousin Bruce. We were picking asparagus, and Bruce found a huge, very long snake (blue racer). He grabbed it by the tail with the sneaky intention of frightening us three girls. He probably would have been very successful, but the snake retaliated on Bruce instead. Bruce was holding it upside down, and it latched on the bottom of his pant leg and would not let go. He was fortunate that he did not receive a big bite since that snake was extremely mad! It took him awhile, but he finally managed to shake it loose and let it go.

As the fields matured and produced more asparagus, my uncle made a three-seated picker to ride on, pulled by his tractor. On these pickers, you had a seat very low to the ground. You straddled the row, and bent over to pick the asparagus. If the rows were real heavy with asparagus, you had to learn to pick very fast. Most everyone soon had a picker of some sort; some propelled by a motor rather than a tractor. It was a much nicer way to pick because you did not have to do all that walking, bending over to pick, and carrying a basket to put the asparagus in which was backbreaking work. As we got older, often just Betty, Ron, Darlene, and I would do the picking. We girls, however, did not think it quite fair since they could tell we picked better than Ron. Ron was an easy going guy and not quite as a thorough of a picker, so they had him drive the tractor. We would have liked to take our turn driving too and have a break from picking.

We had a small asparagus field, also, on the back southeast corner of our farm. A couple of us could get it picked in an hour or so. It never produced a lot of asparagus, however, and Dad decided it was not worth the trips to the canning company five miles away for just a few crates of asparagus. He finally plowed the field under. Later, for many years, we could find some asparagus stalks coming through in the hay field.

After asparagus season, it was soon time to pick cherries. We also did this at Fischers, and later when they got rid of their trees, we picked for a neighbor a little over a mile west from us. Picking cherries was an all day job so we usually packed a lunch for a midday break, or went home for lunch. To pick cherries, we wore a strap or harness over our shoulders with a bucket fastened to it. When our bucket was full, we dumped it in a box called a lug. A lug held twenty-five pounds of cherries and was about thirteen by sixteen inches. We were paid by the lug which was fifty cents a lug for a long time. We had to pick the tree pretty clean and had to climb ladders to do the tops of the tree. I worked as fast and steady as I could but was just an average picker. When we picked at the neighbors, some of the kids were very, very fast and could get a lot of lugs in one day. My future husband and his sisters were known for their fast picking. One sister wanted to set a new record and picked thirty lugs one day. Most picked somewhere between twelve and twenty-four lugs, depending on how abundant the cherries were. Eventually, the price went up to a dollar a lug which was much better pay and pretty good earnings back then.

Since Uncle Henry and Aunt Dorothy had a Christmas tree farm, we often helped plant pine trees. This had to be done by hand. Uncle Henry and his son, Glen, would use a spade and make a big slit in the already made furrows. We followed right behind them with a small gunny sack over our shoulders with the very small trees (about 8 to 10 inches from root to top of the tree). We had to bend over, put the little tree in the slit, and then stamp the dirt closed. Then on to the next slit or hole and plant another tree. We did not seem to mind this job, though we did not do it very frequently. Some days, we worked on our hands and knees in the seed beds weeding the very tiny seedlings. When there was enough help with the planting or weeding, my aunt would grab me to help do housecleaning instead. I did as I was told but really liked working outside better.

Once I was in high school, my job was babysitting. Often on weekends my older sister, Elinor, and husband would have me stay with their two daughters. They lived in New Era only five and a half miles away, but rather than run me home late on a Saturday night, they would just have me spend the night. I would go to church with them on Sunday and then they would bring me home when they visited out at the folks in the afternoon.

Rich and Elinor would also have me stay with them a week or so during the summer, when I was older, to help with the housecleaning. We would work in the morning and often go out to the lake for fun and relax in the afternoons. I think Elinor sometimes thought we worked too hard on the farm and did not have a lot of time to do fun things, so she liked to take me to the lake. And this is something she enjoyed doing too during the hot summer days—to spend afternoons at the lake with some of her lady friends. Rich and Elinor also owned a boat and taught me how to water ski. We did some boating and water skiing some evenings, also.

I know, at times, when we were older we worked pretty hard, but we had time for fun also. We could always get together with cousins or friends in the evenings or on Sunday afternoons. I remember many times walking down to our cousins' house to play kick the can, baseball, or hide and seek in the evenings. One time when I was younger, I was walking home alone from the cousins. It was only about a half mile, but it was always drilled in us to never get in a car with a stranger. I was a bit jumpy walking home alone in the dark that evening and did not have a flashlight along. I heard and saw a car coming in the distance and remember quickly getting in the ditch to hide. I got down on my knees, crouched way down, and tried to make myself less visible. I hoped whoever it was would not see me, held very still, and was very scared. Thankfully, the car kept going down the road. The road was lightly traveled, so most of the time we could make it all the way home without even seeing a car. I arrived home safely though, and usually I was not scared when walking home from the cousins. Sometimes we would be on our bikes and that would have been faster.

I hope this gives the reader a better understanding and awareness of the life, work, and various activities on our small farm. Yes, we often kept busy, but it was a productive and gratifying life. We had time for fun and enjoyment too. You knew your neighbors and were eager to help them if they needed something, and they were always kind and thoughtful to you too. When a lot of the kids went to the same school, and the families often went to the same church, it was just a closer-knit community. People were aware of the needs of friends and neighbors and cared for each other and thought nothing of helping one another. It just was the thing to do.

Dad and Mom often visited with neighbors, relatives, and friends like the Fischers, Vandenbergs, Hecks, Strahls, and in

Muskegon, the Balkemas. Most of the time, Darlene and I needed to go along. We would get rather bored when it turned out to be a very late evening of playing Pinochle or other card games among the adults. We would wind up trying to fall asleep while waiting, but it did not always work out. It was okay at the Hecks, as they had children we could do things with. My folks hardly ever got babysitters for us. If Herb was not home to watch us, a girl down the road, Lorraine, would come to stay with us. I only remember that happening once or twice. Somehow, when Darlene and I were home with Herb, we often would tackle making chocolate fudge. We hardly ever got it right, and it would turn out soft and gooey. But no problem to us—we would divide it up and each have our own section, and then eat it with a spoon.

Looking back, there sure was a lot more visiting back then. You just had more time to do it, and it was something the folks enjoyed doing also. I realize people still get together and visit, but I wonder . . . maybe not as much? I know my husband and I were very involved and busy as our girls got older. There was a lot of running around for sports, music, and social functions. Now some twenty-five or so years later, families are just as busy and probably even more so. They do not have a lot of time for a night of visiting and fun like my folks and others did. Are we missing out on some of that camaraderie with others and with our family? Maybe it would be advantageous to shut off the cell phone, computer, TV and instead call someone up this weekend and have a good old-fashioned visit. You might find it really enjoyable and a fun thing to do!

BRIDGET, CHIEF, MOLLY, RED

A farm means animals; they just go together. I think some of my favorites were our dogs. The dogs always belonged to the whole family. The first dog I remember was a small black and white dog named Tippy, because he had a white tip on his tail. One day, he just disappeared and never showed up to eat; we all felt so sad. We thought maybe he got lost in the woods or something, so on our way to and from school we would call and call him for days and days! He never returned home, so we never knew what happened to him.

Next, we got another small dog, mostly light brown, and named her Topsy. She went everywhere with us: on the wagon when hauling in hay, with us on top of a load of hay bales, in the back of the pick-up truck, or in the cab with us. She was such a nice, sweet dog. It was rather funny since we said she reminded us of our older sister, Elinor. I don't think we ever told Elinor that! We all agreed on this. I think it was because of Topsy's eyes and smile. The poor dog, though, got a bad and lasting ear infection. My folks got some deep purple medicine called Gentian Violet (that would really stain), and we had to put it in her ears to help with the discomfort. This medicine was used as an anti-fungal treatment in ears. Mom did not usually allow pets in the house. However, she felt sorry for Topsy with her sore ears and allowed her, on colder days, to come into the warm kitchen on a rug right by the door. Topsy always was good and stayed right on the rug.

Topsy had a litter of puppies, and we convinced Dad to let us keep one of her pups. I think he consented only because Topsy was getting older, and she was really bothered with that ear infection. He was a cute little brown puppy with white around its neck. We named him King. He was still pretty small when Dad accidentally ran him over with the wheel of the baler. We felt bad as that was the end of King. I do not remember how long we had Topsy, but she was gone for several years before our next dog. Rex just showed up on the front porch one day and looked in the large front picture window when Dad and Mom were sitting in the living room. Dad and Mom kept him. He was a large, black and white dog with long hair. Rex would stand on his hind legs and drink water out of the bird bath. He was a very nice, friendly, loyal dog and a good pet for on the farm. When talking about Rex, there was something comical associated with him. Somehow, when our girls were small they started remembering Grandma and Grandpa Kuipers by linking them up with their dog, Rex. So they became Grandma and Grandpa Rex. Grandma and Grandpa Walhout then got named after their dog at the time, Nicky. One of the girls could not say Nicky clearly and so those grandparents were often called Grandma and Grandpa "Icky."

There were always several cats running around. Once in awhile we could claim a kitten as our own from a litter of kittens. Dad often had to get rid of kittens, or we would have been overpopulated by cats. Once, a mother cat got run over by the tractor which left her kittens. Most of them could lap up the milk from a bowl, but we had to take special care of the runt of the litter. Mom suggested using our doll bottle and trying to get it to drink milk that way. This was an all black cat that someone named Bridget. Anyway, she learned to drink really well from the doll bottle. In fact, she even started holding the bottle with her front paws and could pretty much hold it all on her own! It was such a neat trick that sometimes when we had company, Mom would allow us to bring Bridget in the house and show how she could hold her own bottle and drink the milk. She would still remember how to do this when a grown cat which looked pretty unique!

One time when Dad was mowing hay, he had the misfortune of hitting and killing a mother rabbit. You always had to watch for animals, especially fawns hiding in the hay so you would not hit them. You would often find snakes in the hay fields, also, so it was not unusual when loading the hay bales to find a dead blue racer in the bale. When Dad killed the mother rabbit, he found five or six tiny little bunnies in a nest. He felt sorry for them, because he knew they were too little to fend for themselves. Dad brought them home, but they were so tiny Mom figured the only way to try and keep them alive was to use rags, dip the rags in warm milk and try to get the tiny, tiny bunnies to suck some milk from the saturated rags. We would get them to take a little and would repeat this process about every three or four hours. My mom even got up during the night to do the feedings, and she would try to get them to eat during a couple feedings when we were in school. They were kept in a box in the kitchen to keep them warm. But, though we tried hard to keep them alive, they all died after a few days.

Often, on the farm, we would have a horse. My older brother, Don, had a beautiful horse named Chief. I do not remember this horse really, considering that I was only three years old, except for seeing it in pictures. Chief was a smart and special horse. Don used to ride him to school one mile away and tie him to a post all day, then ride him back home. Some people, though, started to complain about the horse droppings on the school yard. So Don rode him to school, let him loose, and Chief would trot home. He probably was good about it for he knew a warm barn and food were waiting for him when he got home. Dad would keep an eye out for him and let him in the barn when he arrived home. It must have looked funny, however, when Chief ran down the road without a rider. If anyone would have met him in a car, they would have wondered what was going on! I'm sure, sometimes, Chief would just cut across the fields. Don would have had to walk home when school was done for the day. He said Chief could pull a cutter and buggy also, though he was a horse for riding. He even was used to cultivate at times.

The next horse was a gentle, smaller workhorse named Molly. Molly was used for cultivating corn, and she was used in the garden too before we owned a rototiller. I remember helping with this sometimes and I would lead her between the rows while Dad operated the cultivator. That was a help to Dad since he did not have to steer Molly then and could concentrate on the cultivating. Herb told me that Uncle Henry borrowed her some too. Molly also could be hooked up for buggy rides and sleigh rides. Herb remembers taking many relatives for buggy rides. He also hooked Molly up to a friend's buckboard for a Sunday ride with friends and cousins. Another time on a sleigh ride, he said he came in the driveway too fast and tipped over with Molly and the overturned sleigh continuing on to the barn. Herb and the others remained lying on the drive but no one was hurt. One evening, a large group of school kids met at the top of the hill by the school for a sliding party. They built a nice bonfire on the hill where we could get warmed up. Herb came with Molly and the sleigh and gave some rides also. What a fun evening!

You could ride Molly some, but she was a bit wide since she was a workhorse. One day, I tried riding her bareback. We were trotting when I started sliding and slid right off her. When I fell, I landed right by her, and she stepped heavily on my leg by my right ankle. I still have an indent where she trampled me! We also used Molly to drive six to eight cows, but sometimes more, to the pasture on our 80 acres a mile away. We would have to do this before school and then again after school bring the cows back home. Darlene and I would have to do this, and on occasion, some friends (who lived close by) thought this was fun and would come along to help. Sometimes, the cows would give us problems along the road and try to sneak in to the neighbors' fields. When we put the cows in the fenced-in pasture on the 80, Molly was turned in the pasture to graze also.

Mom or Dad would pick us up with the car, after this chore of herding the cows was done and bring us to school. We did not have to do this during the wintertime. Then the cows either were in the barn or in the pasture on the home 40 acres. One time when Dad or Mom dropped us off to herd the cows home, the cows and Molly were a long way back in the pasture. Finally, I got Molly and managed to climb on her bare back and was going to drive the cows to the gate. For some reason, Molly decided to meander over and enjoy the wide creek with me riding her. I could not make her obey, as I possibly did not have her bridle on yet. Maybe Molly decided she wanted to cool off and stood in the middle of the creek stomping her hoofs to splash the water up, getting us both wet. I tried and tried, to no avail, to make her climb out of the creek. I was in a pickle and did not know what to do. Finally, I guess she decided she had enough and clambered up out of the creek. We gathered the cows, and could head home.

The next horse we had was the riding horse of Herb's. His name was Red because of his brownish red color. This was during my later grade school years and early high school years. Herb was busy working on another farm, so I rode Red the most. My cousins, down the road from us, would board a couple of horses for a riding stable during their off season (wintertime), so they would have horses to ride. My cousin, Betty, and I were out riding one day in the wintertime. On the way home from our ride, we decided to race from the corner to Betty's house. Her horse, however, decided to turn in our drive instead which came first, as it was used to going there often. We were going too fast to make the driveway, and her horse slipped on some snow and fell. The horse was all right, but Betty wound up with a broken leg out of the accident. I remember her dad was not happy that it had happened and sort of blamed me, since I had suggested we race! But perhaps it was better Betty got the broken leg and not the horse. When a horse broke a leg, it would often have to be shot. Being they were boarding the two horses, they probably would have had to pay for the loss of a horse.

There was another small mishap with Red. One day, I got the idea I wanted to try Red hitched to an old buggy we still had. Dad helped me hitch him up being I could not have figured it out all by myself. I am rather surprised Dad went along with my idea not knowing what Red was going to do when in a harness. We got Red hitched up, and down the road I went. It was fun riding along in the buggy, and the horse behaved quite well so he must have been trained to pull; but, I am pretty sure this was the first time we tried him. All was going well, and I went three or four miles down the road. But then, on the way back, a car went by us and spooked Red. He took off, and I had a hard time getting him to slow down. Somehow, we ended up tangled in some brush in the ditch. It broke some of the harness and something on the buggy tongue. It was broken bad enough that I could not get the buggy home. I unhitched Red and rode bareback up to my uncle and aunt's on the hill a mile away and phoned Dad from there. He had to bring the trailer or something to haul the buggy home. I never hooked Red up to the buggy again and just stuck to riding him, which I really enjoyed. I frequently would take a long ride and get off to walk for awhile for a break. I could just leave the reins on the saddle horn, and Red would just follow right behind me. I felt bad when later on Red had the misfortune of getting the heaves and we eventually had to get rid of him. Heaves is a bad cough and occasionally Red would have trouble breathing. It often occurs in horses more than six years of age and can be caused by mold or dust (Red was then around seventeen years).

Poor Red would cough so much you could not even ride him anymore. Red was the last of our horses.

So we usually always had cows, calves, chickens, dogs, and cats around on the farm. We grew up liking animals and knew how to take care of them. Dad raised pigs for meat, occasionally beef cattle, some turkeys once, but I cannot remember ever having goats or sheep. You did not have to have a garbage disposal since either the pigs or chickens would gladly eat the garbage you tossed to them. Dogs and cats would get any scraps left on someone's plate after a meal. The cows thought it was a great treat when cornstalks from the garden were cut down and tossed to them over the fence. I remember having a steer once that I raised as my own. He was a nice pet. Sometimes it was hard to have a pet like that butchered or even when the chickens were killed, it was a bit sad for us. But then there were the dirty, grunting pigs that I never liked, so I did not mind that their purpose was to eventually wind up on the table for food.

SPIDER, ROOT CELLAR, BEES

One of the special things when growing up was when we purchased our first TV. My brother, Herb, said it was right around 1952 when we got the first set and remembers watching *Howdy Doody* and some Westerns. I recall cartoons, *Mickey Mouse Club,* and we often watched the old Alfred Hitchcock scary movies. He reminded me of going to watch TV with our cousins on their small set occasionally. It then came to my mind also, how their set had a problem which caused the whole picture to always rotate up. They could not get it adjusted to quit rolling, but we still would try and watch the picture. Our eyes would get so tired going down and then following the picture up, then down and up again . . . over and over! But we would keep at it until the movie or program was done. Now that I think of it, it was rather funny.

Another TV occurrence I remember is when Herb would stay home from church Sunday nights to do the evening milking and chores. Sometimes my folks allowed Darlene and me to stay home too, when we were little. Darlene and I liked watching *Lassie,* which came on Sunday nights, but Herb wanted to watch *The Cisco Kid.* Our parents told us to take turns, which sounded like the fair thing to do. However, sometimes when it was our turn to watch *Lassie,* Herb had manipulated the channel control knob somehow. When we tried putting it on the channel for *Lassie, The Cisco Kid* came on instead! We would be so disappointed!

My parents never went to movies nor did they ever take us to see one. One evening when I was about eleven or twelve, my aunt Dorothy thought she would do something really special and take her two sons (both older than me) and me to a movie. I was so excited about going to a real movie in a real theater; my very first one! I never quite figured out, however, why she took us to this particular movie, unless her sons had persuaded her that they wanted to see it. I cannot remember the name of it, but this man would turn into a real frightening hairy beast of some sort. I still see this scene in my mind quite clearly. The man was climbing up the brick wall of a tall house with vines on it, in the dark, and he started growing hair all over his face, arms, and hands. To me, he was terrifying and horrendous! Not at all what a little girl wanted to see. If I remember right, he would climb into windows and kill people too. I did not enjoy this movie at all! And I do not think I went to a movie again until I was in college and went to "The Sound of Music." Now that was a great movie!

Sometimes, scary things were found closer to home. One evening Darlene and I were both upstairs in our own bedrooms, getting ready for bed. All of a sudden, out of the corner of my eye I saw movement, and there crawling across the floor was a very, very huge ugly spider! I quickly hopped on my bed and called Darlene from the next room. She came in my bedroom, took one look at it, and went downstairs to tell Dad of our dilemma. Dad hardly ever came upstairs, so here he came up the stairs, grumbling all the way . . . and saying, "You silly girls afraid of a teeny little spider and making me come all the way up here to kill a tiny little spider." That statement was barely out of his mouth when he saw the furry thing and said, "Oh, that is a big spider!" He proceeded to whack it several times to kill it. Thankfully, he killed it and did not miss it, or I would not have wanted to sleep upstairs that night. Growing up on the farm we were used to bees, insects, and spiders, but I still did not want huge ones in my bedroom!

October meant Halloween and we always really looked forward to it. When growing up in the country, we did not ride in cars and go to heavy populated city streets like youngsters do now, getting lots of treats at house after house. We just walked for miles and miles around a block to neighbors who lived far apart from each other. Then we would hit another block and have to walk a long ways again. Sometimes, we would cut across fields in the dark to hit a couple more houses. We did not obtain huge bags full of treats like kids do today, but we certainly received plenty. What we did gather was worthwhile. There were nice full-size large candy bars, homemade fudge, gum, caramel apples, or maybe popcorn balls. We knew most of the people where we stopped, and we were not worried about getting anything contaminated or tainted. The kids I went with did not play any mean tricks; we just had fun trick-or-treating. It would be a little scary sometimes stumbling across some fields or climbing over fences in the dark.

This next story is perhaps a little more unusual than scary, but to Darlene and me, it was definitely frightening also. Mom and Dad had some neighbors over to visit during the daytime. This was a nice, friendly older couple who lived three-fourths of a mile away. They had visited and were saying their goodbyes outside of the kitchen door on the steps of the entry way. All of a sudden, Mr. Southworth had what they thought was a heart attack. He died right there at the base of those steps. Somehow, they managed to carry him into the house and lay him on the living room couch. They could see it was fatal and called the hearse to pick him up. Darlene and I were home at the time and probably just went upstairs to our rooms for awhile. It is odd how something like that affects children. We would not sit on that couch for the longest time!

Telling about some fearful things, an incident happened to me by our root cellar. This root cellar was located off to the side of our backyard. There was an era when many neighbors, including us, put in these cellars. My older brother, Don, said that when they still lived in Muskegon, they used to practice for air raids and would have to shut their lights off. World War II was over, but people still had it on their minds and may have been worried about bombs and thought cellars were the answer. People built the root cellars to be used for storage also, and for safety in event of tornadoes. Don helped Dad make our cellar probably in the late 1940s or maybe 1950. This was partially underground, and you went down about eight small steps to get into it. It kept fruits and vegetables from freezing during the winter months and kept produce cool during summer months, preventing spoilage. We stored apples, potatoes, squash, turnips, carrots, beets, cabbage, and onions in it. Besides this produce, sometimes mice found a way to crawl into the cellar. One day, my mom told me to bring one of the cats down in the cellar to catch the annoying critters. I started down the steps with the cat, opened the door, and for some reason the cat got spooked about going in the cellar. She started clawing up my shirt and right onto my face, making a deep gouge with her claw right under my eye as she jumped to freedom. The scratch hurt but healed up just fine.

Talking about storing food leads into my mom's idea of making homemade root beer. She read up on how to do it and got the necessary equipment and ingredients for making it. I remember helping her some in the basement. We really liked this root beer! It was more like root beer Kool-Aid that you once could buy. She used to store all these bottles of root beer in the attic since it needed a warm place to ferment. It would take many weeks before it was ready. Sometimes the caps would not hold, and you would hear a pop in the attic and knew another bottle of root beer had exploded. She did this for several years, and then gave it up. It was a lot of extra work and sometimes made a mess in the attic.

We also had our own honey for awhile. My older brother Don said they were his bees since he had them for a project for a high school agriculture class. He got some hives and bees from Grandpa Fischer. Grandpa had bees and hives on his place since he enjoyed tending bees and harvesting the honey. Grandpa helped Don with his bees, some. I remember how they would get dressed up in heavy coats, real thick gloves, and hats with netting around it. The netting would keep the bees from stinging on the face or neck. Don would put dry sumac in a closed container and set it on fire; it had bellows on it that blew the smoke at the bees. This would make the bees a little sluggish and kept them out of his way while he removed the frames of wax and honey. Then, the honeycombs would be brought in the house to remove the honey.

I don't know if they bought an extractor or borrowed it from Grandpa. I do not remember this, but my brother said the extractor was in our shed. This extractor was placed in the middle of a large tub. You would fasten one of the wax combs to the spinner in the middle of the tub. It was then spun fast so the honey flew out and into the tub. After extracting the honey, Mom could put it in any container she wished and store it in the cupboards. You did not have to can it as it was naturally preserved. Sometimes, we would just break a piece off from the honeycomb when it was brought in and suck out the honey. It was delicious! Honey was one more thing we had of our own and did not have to buy at the grocery store. It sure helped on the grocery bills when you had your own fruits, vegetables, eggs, meats, chicken, milk, grape juice, root beer, and the honey.

My folks had another endeavor which was growing raspberries, and they sold them for many years. I think they rather enjoyed it, and it was a little extra income. They had many rows, and it took a long time to pick them all. Dad would help Mom pick when he could, we kids would help, and after we were older and out of the house, a neighbor lady often came to help. Dad made little carriers that we could tie around our waists which would hold two pint boxes side by side. We would sort as we picked. If there were berries with a blemish or not quite perfect, they would go in the pint box that we would keep for ourselves. The perfect and beautiful berries were sold. Friends and others would call and place their orders, and my folks would fill the orders as the berries were ready. Half a case (twelve pints) was twelve dollars, and a full case (twenty-four pints) was twenty-four dollars. Back then it seemed like pretty good money, but they are much more expensive when you buy them in stores or at farmer markets today! We could pick berries off the same row for many years, but Dad was always setting out new rows too. When the older rows were not producing as well anymore, new rows were ready for harvesting. A neighbor had a spray rig pulled behind his tractor that was used for spraying his fruit trees. Once or twice a season, he would spray my folks' raspberry bushes which kept them free of any unwanted pests.

Mom could sew, too, and that was another way to help out on the expenses. I know she sewed dresses, aprons, pillow cases, or other items but she did not have a whole lot of extra time for sewing. She did a lot of mending, though, and kept our clothes repaired. In her older and not so busy years, Mom loved to make afghans and made many, many of them! She was always asking people to buy the yarn, and she would crochet an afghan for them. We still use many of her beautiful and serviceable afghans around our house to this day. My daughters have some around their homes also, which is a nice memory of their grandma.

I thought of one more thing Mom did . . . when she was a grandma. Mom was not afraid to try new things; she had a rather adventurous spirit. Snowmobiling became popular in the late 1960s. My husband was into it before we started dating. Then some of our first dates were snowmobiling, riding double on one machine. It did not take me long to really enjoy the sport (and the person driving the snowmobile)! My mom expressed an interest in going on a ride once to see what snowmobiling was all about. So one sunny and beautiful winter day, I took her for a ride. I led with one machine, and she followed driving her own snowmobile. I would turn around and check on her, and she would be all smiles. I thought that was admirable since she was already sixty-five years old or more at the time!

SWAMP, SLIDING, GET-TOGETHERS

For a country girl, winters meant hours of outdoor play and lots of fun. On our property, right behind the barn, was a swamp. There was not a lot of value in the swamp except my dad pumped water out of it during the summer to sprinkle the garden. He figured it was a good way to save on water from our well, and the water in the swamp was just sitting there anyway. Also, he thought the swamp water was better for the garden than the very cold water from the well. He maybe was right since he could always grow a magnificent and superb garden! With the swamp quite close, it was nice to hear the chorus of frogs singing in the evenings: a sound I love to this day. I do not think this swamp was any deeper than two to three feet in most places, and there was usually water in it year round. The swamp turned to ice during the winter making it a magical and enchanting play area. As kids, my two cousins, Darlene, and I found it was a wonderful place to spend many interesting hours. There were a lot of bushes growing all about in the swamp, but there was a place in the middle where we could shovel the snow off for ice-skating. I loved roller-skating, but never was very good at ice-skating. I thought maybe my ankles were too weak, but thinking back, it was more likely that the ice skates were no good at giving support. The skates were very old and well used! Besides skating, we spent more of our time in the bushes. We would break off pieces of brush to make paths through it, make forts and houses, find secret passage ways through the brush, and just had all kinds of fun! We would spend hours and hours out there as we always dressed plenty warm. I think our discovered play area on the swamp was pretty unique, and I doubt if many other kids came up with the idea of playing on a swamp. A plus for our parents: they did not worry about us breaking through the ice or drowning since it was not very deep.

Another very favorite thing to do in the winter was slide downhill. I remember being pretty happy when I got my new sled called the "Radio Flyer." It was a wooden sled with runners and worked the best on hard packed snow or when there was a hard crust on top. We did not use much else for sliding except maybe a piece of sheet metal we found in the garage. Darlene remembers having a sled she used that Dad made out of some piece of metal, making it round like a saucer. And my husband recalls sliding on a "Norge Tin" which was just an old Norge refrigerator door. Norge refrigerators were made from 1930 through 1970 right in Muskegon, thirty miles away.

One particular day was really good sliding as the snow had a hard crust, and you could slide right on top. We were sliding on the hill across the road from our house. Somehow, Darlene, the two cousins, and I came up with the idea of all four of us piling on top of each other on my sled. I was the oldest so was on the bottom, and the other three piled on top of me all lying on our stomachs. It all went well until we slid to the bottom of the hill, and the runners cut through the snow as we slowed down! We all slid forward off the sled, and I could not hold my head up with three kids on top of me, weighing my face down. I got many scrapes from the crusty snow on one cheek, on my nose, and around my eye. I walked home a bleeding mess! Mom cleaned me up and had me lie down and rest on the couch. I know it hurt and smarted for several days, and I looked pretty bad. Everyone asked, "What happened to you?" I was in grade school when this happened.

A very good sliding hill was in the field just beyond our cousins'. We would often spend hours there sliding down that short hill over and over again! I still remember one winter day when the snowflakes were softly and lazily coming down in large amounts. After sliding for awhile, we all laid on our sleds enjoying the beauty. We were lying on our backs, looking straight up into all that softly cascading snow coming down gently on our faces. I can still envision its grandeur and beauty. We were experiencing and witnessing God's wondrous handiwork! Other times, we would go a little farther east and slide on a big hill right on the road. The traffic was very light, so we did not have to worry much about cars. The trouble with that hill was you would slide so far that you would have a long, long walk back up the hill! Sometimes, when stopping at the cousins' house on the way home from our sliding adventures, their mother would give us a 'fresh from the oven' baked loaf of bread. Mmm, we could smell it as we walked home and always were eager to eat it. Her homemade bread (along with my mom's) was the very best!

Tobogganing also was an exciting and fun adventure. My brother, Herb, owned an eight-foot toboggan. One Saturday, Herb and his wife, brother Don and his wife, and I drove to this very huge hill a couple miles away. It is high enough to be a small mountain. To have that high hill right there in the middle, with the flat land all around it, is quite unusual. It is probable a glacier moved across that area and made that little mountain erupt. Since it was so high, you could really sail down fast! On one trip down, we could not avoid this fairly good-sized tree and went right over it, causing us to go airborne, and then we all fell off the toboggan. It was quite funny! Then came the long climb back up the mountain. Recently, we were across the road visiting the owner of that huge, huge hill. It has been about sixty years since we went tobogganing there, and the small mountain is now totally covered by trees. No more tobogganing on there for anyone. When we would take our own children sliding on a couple favorite hills, my husband would spoil the girls. They would slide down the hill, and then he would let them hop on behind him on the snowmobile (pulling their sleds along) and bring them back up the hill. They liked that method of getting back up the hills a lot!

One more winter thing we did for at least two years was have catechism classes in our homes. My folks got together with some neighbors and came up with the idea. Rather than traveling to town when the roads were often bad, why not meet in the neighboring homes for catechism. Catechism is a summary of Christian doctrine, in question and answer form, and taught to children and young people. There were four families involved, all within a mile radius, and all belonged to the same church. Each family would take their turns having everyone over. They got the catechism books from our church, and the moms were the teachers. We divided up with two or three in each class. The dads came along too and visited while we were having our lesson. Of course, after our lessons, we would have food. They were all good cooks, but one neighbor especially made very delicious sloppy joes! They did not have the canned Manwich Sloppy Joe sauce so this was all made from scratch. Mrs. Heck even had carrots cut up fine in it, which was probably a way to stretch the hamburger. But it made it taste really great! Darlene and I often bring up about Stena Heck's very delicious sloppy joes. I have added carrots a few times when I make sloppy joes, but my family just does not think that carrots should be in it. Everyone has different tastes, and I think the fine, diced carrots are great in sloppy joes.

When we were in high school, we had to walk from our house up to the corner to catch the school bus. My cousins and another family had to do this too, and we all met at the intersection to wait for the bus. The bad thing during the wintertime is it could get very cold standing there waiting (and there was no shelter). Infrequently, the bus could run late if the roads were bad because of the snow conditions. Schools back then never canceled because of poor roads! Maybe a very few times they would not send the buses out, but they still would have school. Then the kids that rode the bus would have to make up the work they missed. When I attended high school and for many years after that, the girls were required to wear dresses or skirts and blouses. The only exception was once a month on Friday they would have slacks day, and then the next Monday they would have dress-up day. I looked forward to wearing slacks but not my Sunday best on Monday. Anyway, one cold winter morning when the bus was running very late, we had to stand out in the cold for a long time and unfortunately several of us were wearing skirts. I discovered I actually got some frostbite on my legs and those spots of discoloration would show up on my legs for a very long time afterward. We should have thought and slipped slacks on under our skirts until we reached school that day, but we did not know the bus was going to run so late.

Kuipers' 9 Children; Aunt Annie Far Left, Our Dad Far Right

Don and Dad (has hat on) With a Load of Hay

About 1930, Dad and Mom

Mom in Her Fur Coat Holding Judy (1945)

Dad and Judy (1945)

1946, Herb & Judy

Judy in Scarf, Herb and Cousins, Glen & Bruce

Chief (the Horse), Don and Judy (3 yrs.)

Judy when 4 or 5 yrs.

Judy & Darlene at Christmas (about 2 & 6 yrs.)

My Mom, a Fantastic Cook!

(1949), Elinor, Darlene 8 mo., Dad & Mom, Don, Herb 7 yrs., Judy 4 yrs.

(1953), Don & Arlene's Wedding, Judy Far Left and Darlene in Front

Judy, 8 Years

Doughnuts Hanging to Dry on Carrom Sticks

Mom With Her Dad, Grandpa Fischer

The Kuipers' Farm (Picture taken about 1951)

The Kuipers' Farmhouse

Judy's Bedroom

Horse (Red), Darlene and Judy

Rex, The Dog That Came to Stay

ACCIDENTS, MISHAPS, LIGHTNING

E arlier, I told about how I tipped over the tractor while mowing hay. My brother, Herb, remembers rolling the tractor several times. The first time for him, he was plowing a newly cleared field on our 80 acres and got too close to a ditch and rolled the tractor. A neighbor close to the 80 helped pull it back up, and Herb drove it home. Another time, he was custom baling (that is when someone else hired a person with a baler to bale their hay) and on his second round a bale had rolled too far. The left back wheel hit the bale as he came around and rolled the tractor, but the hitch kept it from rolling all the way over. The field owner pulled it back up, and Herb had to get the baler hitch straightened.

I have frequently mentioned about the 80 acres we owned. Writing about it made me want to see it once again. It is owned by someone else now, but we knew they would not mind if we visited the property. We live four miles from the 80 now; my husband and I each hopped on a tractor and drove out. My husband enjoys restoring old tractors and has four of them. He is a John Deere man, but he restored a Farmall also. That is the one I like to drive, though I am a little partial to Allis Chalmers since that is what I always drove on our farm. I went down memory lane as we drove around on the property, except it was hard to get to some of the fields. We could easily drive on two of the larger hay fields still being farmed by a man that lives across the road from the property. He is presently renting the two larger fields. The little two-track back to some of the smaller fields where we used to grow hay is not passable anymore. There are trees and bushes growing on the path so we walked to two of the smaller fields. Pine trees planted between these hay fields once were used for Christmas trees and now are some thirty feet tall. I felt some nostalgia standing in those fields again!

The most impressive trees are the large stand of red pines on the northwest corner of the property. There they are yet . . . standing so stately, magnificent, and tall! I think some must be sixty feet tall and measure three and a half feet around (I used a tape measure to measure a few of the trunks). They had room for good growth as my dad had a few loads of logs taken out and sold for pulpwood. I am surprised the present owner does not sell some of the trees since red pines can be used for lumber, cabin logs, posts, and utility poles. I read that red pines can grow from sixty-five to one hundred feet tall and two to three feet in diameter. Red pines are native to Michigan, so are relatively free of major insects and diseases. Dad sold this property after he was retired. He asked his children first if anyone wanted to buy it. We were not financially in the position to do that then with raising our family of four girls. I was like Dad and really appreciated and cherished those private and somewhat secluded 80 acres with the beautiful rolling hills, creek, and pine trees. I also could envision a house on the hill overlooking the creek. What a nice piece of property to be able to hike around on, enjoy the wildlife, and witness God's creation. I really wish we could still purchase it, but it is not for sale.

So not only were there the tractor accidents, but 'the load of hay' mishaps. I remember one time, after loading most of the wagon with hay bales on the 80, we had to go down a steep grade from one hay field to the next. Dad was driving the tractor and half of the bales slid forward and off as we went down that short, steep incline. Not a lot of fun to have to reload them! To load the bales off the fields, you had a tractor driver and, ideally, a couple people or more to toss the bales up on the wagon. Also, one or more stacking the bales properly on the wagon. If you were short of help, you would put the tractor in a low gear and have it travel very slowly on its own (no driver). You just nudged the steering wheel every so often to make the tractor go where you wanted it to while walking alongside, loading the bales. It was during my early teenage years when Dad bought a baler with a long chute on the back. This chute was about the same height as the wagon, so you pulled the wagon behind the baler while baling the hay. The hay bales would get pushed out the long chute, right onto the wagon. Then you only needed one person on the wagon to stack the bales. To make it easier for us, Darlene and I would do this job together while Dad drove the tractor and baled the hay. Oftentimes, I stacked the load of bales by myself. Hay bales were heavy bales, on an average of forty pounds a bale. Of course, depending on the hay conditions and how you set the baler, they could be heavier or lighter. At least that long chute made loading hay easier since you did not have to pick up the bales off the field and toss them on the wagon. Hay wagons were right around three feet high. As a youngster, that was pretty high to throw a heavy bale up on the wagon!

One day we were hauling a load of hay bales from the 80, and I think our cousins were with us also. We were all sitting on top of this full wagonload of bales. When it was a full load, the bales were stacked quite high. As often as I had to load hay wagons, I should remember how many layers high the bales were, but probably right around seven tiers high. We had fun riding on the top on the way home, relaxing, after working hard to load the hay bales. My dad was driving, and we were going down the road when the wagon started whipping back and forth going down a big hill. All of a sudden, bales started separating and falling off, and we lost almost all of the load, along with us kids falling with the bales. We were dazed a bit but no one got hurt! Then we had to reload that load and get the bales off the road before a car came.

Before we had the baler with the chute, we had to get neighbors, cousins, brother Don, and whoever we could to help get the hay hauled in, especially if it was threatening rain. Dad was still working in Muskegon at the factory. It is important to get the hay under cover while it is still dry. The hay for the animals is fresher and more wholesome if it does not get wet. Another important reason to get it in the barn while it's still dry is that hay packed tightly in a bale can get so hot if it is damp, it could start a fire and consequently a barn fire. Dad was always very careful about this. We had three neighbors, on the same road, within about three miles have the misfortune of their barns burning down. Two were from lightning strikes, and one was from either damp hay getting too hot or a hot tractor starting some sparks. I know Dad had some pretty, decorative, blue metal lightning rods on the barn and on the house. Whether they really helped protect the structure from a lightning strike, I do not know, but maybe so.

The best thing about haying was after working a couple hours after supper loading hay either at home or helping the neighboring cousins, the treat was going swimming at Fogg Lake four miles away. It was a smaller lake with no houses built on it. At the little beach where we went swimming, the lake bottom was clean with no grasses, cattails, or bulrushes growing. The father of my cousins, Marinus, would load us up and drive us since we were younger then and could not drive ourselves. How cool and refreshing that was after a hard day of work! We always so looked forward to that, and sometimes, there would be quite a bunch of us. We have very fond memories of Fogg Lake and swimming there. We went there much more often than Lake Michigan, which was only fifteen miles away. If you go back to Fogg Lake now, there are several houses built on it, and it does not look like they use our spot for swimming anymore. It would not be as private with houses close by.

Another mishap with a load of hay bales was when it had started to rain, and we had a load of hay sitting in the yard. Dad told Darlene to quickly pull the tractor and wagon into the lower part of the barn, tractor first since there was room for both the tractor and the load of bales. She had to take it down a steep little hill, and she hit the brakes too hard going down the hill. A bunch of bales slid forward pushing Darlene's face hard against the steering wheel. She still has a small impression on her face from that mishap.

One more thing about haying. I can vaguely remember when they used to load loose hay with a hay elevator picking up the windrows. The elevator was pulled behind the tractor and wagon (earlier years with horses). At the barn, it was unloaded with a huge two-prong steel fork called a grappling hook, or some called it a grab fork. This was on the end of a thick and heavy rope hooked on the barn roof beam, and it grabbed huge clumps of hay at a time. The tractor (before the tractor, a horse) was used to pull the rope and lift the huge clump of hay up with a pulley system to the hayloft or haymow. Someone had to work inside of the barn also, to trip the fork and spread the clumps of hay around with pitchforks. I was very young when they had to do it that way.

Once, my dad had a bad accident in the barn. There was a trap door up in the loft where the hay and straw bales were stored. Dad was tossing the straw down for bedding for the cattle below. He slipped, fell through the trap door, and broke some ribs. He was in such pain from the broken ribs! Whenever he got in or out of a chair, he would holler out in pain. We dreaded when he went to bed at night as again, he would cry out in pain. We felt so bad for him.

I remember brother Herb getting a terrible gash in his leg from an ax accident. He said he was with some of his friends trying to make a cabin near a swamp by his friend's place. They were cutting logs when Herb missed and hit his leg. I remember seeing the gash so deep that bone was showing, but my mom doctored it and did not even bring him in to see a doctor. Herb remembers putting another rather large hole in one of his lower legs. The bike he was learning to ride was Elinor's old one. It did not have a pedal on one side but just a cut off bolt sticking out. Herb's foot slipped off and the bolt cut into his leg. He said it was deeper than the ax misfortune.

Thinking about these unforeseen happenstances, it is a wonder there were not more of them. I am thinking of a game Darlene, my cousins, and I would play, and it was like the game Twister. We would use a knife from the kitchen or an old hunter's knife (it was not too sharp!), and toss it trying to get the blade to stick in the ground. A person would have to put his foot there and another person would get a turn with the knife and so on. We must have been fairly good since I do not remember anyone getting stabbed in the foot. So yes, the game was similar to the modern game of Twister only we used a knife!

Also, there was an accident that happened in our neighborhood—it was a tragedy and so very sad. Friends of my folks lived one road to the south of us and a few miles away. This older couple enjoyed fishing and often fished on a little lake (Mud Lake) not far from their home. I did not quite remember just how it happened, so today my husband asked a ninety-seven-year-old friend from the neighborhood (with an excellent memory) how it happened. He said Carl had just made an anchor of cement in a bucket and was using it that day when fishing. When they were ready to quit and go home, he had trouble pulling up the anchor. It had caught on some of the pond weeds and grass on the bottom of the lake, and Carl struggled to free it. In this process, first he almost tipped over the small boat, and then he wound up slipping and falling in. Sadly, he got tangled in the reed grass and bulrushes and drowned. What a thing for his poor wife in the boat to witness—maybe not knowing where he was or not able to swim herself. We heard that she sat in the boat and hollered and hollered for help. Either someone living close to the lake heard her or someone passing by finally came and rescued her. What a terrible thing for her to go through!

My parents too had some troubled times with sadness and heartaches. I mentioned before how my dad rarely came up the stairs to our bedrooms. But one day when I was in high school, Dad came up the stairs very early in the morning. Right away we wondered what was wrong. He had to deliver the sad news that our uncle and aunt were both killed in a car accident. Uncle Bill was my mom's youngest brother. Bill and Helen drove a small Volkswagen Beetle and had been in the area visiting. They resided in Battle Creek which was over a couple hours away. One day, they were still in the area and going down the highway when an oncoming car passed someone on the right side. When they were pulling back on the highway, the car caught the edge of the pavement, and swerved right in the path of my uncle and aunt hitting them head-on. It was a very sad thing to happen.

We always remembered this unfortunate happening and thus felt unsafe in smaller cars. Another uncle (and an older brother of my mom's) finally did buy a smaller car, a Volkswagen station wagon. He almost always just drove it locally after what had happened to his brother. I am not sure when, but maybe about ten years later, that uncle and aunt were also tragically killed in a car accident in their smaller car. This time, a young teenage boy had reached down to pick up something off the floor of his car. In that short instant of not keeping his eyes on the road, he swerved and hit my uncle and aunt head-on and they both were killed. Hard to believe it could have happened to both couples in the same way and both couples had no children.

It maybe is a bit unusual to include these happenings in a book, but they are things that happened and memories of when we were growing up on the farm. I might add that on life's journey there are ups and downs, times of joy and times of sadness, certainties and uncertainties, times of happiness and times of sorrow, smooth times and troubled times, and as we have often heard, "In everyone's life, some rain must fall." But after the rain, there are the rainbows reminding us of God's faithfulness and promises. He is always there for us, and He will see us through the troubled times. He is right beside us to provide comfort, to guide, to protect, and to lead us along life's journey.

Some may ask, "How do we know this?" We can sense God's presence when reading His Word, when praying, in church during worship, when we hear someone's testimony, when we hear Christian songs and hymns, in nature, and in the beauty of creation. We sense Him in the miracle of the birth of a baby, in answered prayers, or in the times of need, during life's struggles, sense Him in the examples of other Christian lives, and when we hear that 'still small voice.' He is there when you see evidence of lives changed, when someone repents of their sins, and turns to God and wants to live for Him! If you are someone who has never known God's presence in your life, do not wait until it is too late. Find a good Bible-believing church or seek out a Christian person to help you find God's way and will for your life. There is a judgment day coming and then it is too late.

Many memories continue to come to mind, so after relating some sad ones, I will include more lighthearted ones as they come drifting in my thoughts randomly. I reminisce on how it was a treat for us kids to sit in the living room and eat supper on TV trays and watch TV. Or during the times of bad lightning storms, Dad would have us come down from upstairs, and we would all watch the storm sitting in the living room. We did have some bad storms too, so I was scared enough to come down! Once the neighbor's barn was struck by lightning and burned down, and we saw it all happen. This was the farm where our cousins used to live but by then had moved away. Also, my parents used to tell about lightning that danced across the floor in the front room.

My mom said Elinor was washing dishes once at the kitchen sink during a storm and got a burn mark on her stomach, where she was leaning against the edge of the counter. The counter top had a metal strip running along the edge and the lightning charge followed it.

I think about a few times when my sister and I would be fighting and arguing, and Mom would put us to work on washing windows on opposite sides . . .of the same window. It would not be long and we would be laughing at each other and the argument all forgotten.

Darlene and I were always listening to our 45 speed records on our little record player upstairs. We had lots of records: Gene Autry records, Christmas and Easter records, hymns, and cute kids' records. During my teenage years, I preferred calm music and not rock and roll. I had *Rambling Rose* by Nat King Cole, *Precious and Few*, *Cherish*, *There's Nothing I Can Say* by Rick Nelsen, *Sealed With a Kiss*, and *Bridge Over Troubled Waters*. Perry Como was one of my favorites.

Going with Dad to a cattle auction also comes to mind. Darlene and I had fun riding in the pick-up truck with him to a town forty-four miles away. At the auction barn, you could walk on the catwalks above all the stalls where the cattle, pigs, and horses were kept until they were auctioned off. Once in awhile Dad would bring a calf or pig to be auctioned off, and other times he would be looking for a calf or steer to buy. We went in the evening. They always had this auction once a month on a certain night of the week.

One nice summer day I got an idea and decided to go ahead and tackle a big project. I guess I was thinking it was improving the looks of our yard but did not think to get permission first, in case my parents did not wish to have it done. We had two larger pine trees on the home property, one in the front yard and one in front of the garage. Then we also had at least a half dozen or more smaller pines in the yard to the west of the house. Anyway, for some reason, I got it in my head to trim off all the lower branches of the pines and set to work. It was a lot of work, too, with so many trees, and the larger trees had very huge branches. When maybe I was halfway done with my job, Dad came home and asked what was I doing! He did not really say he did not like it, and I could not leave the project half finished, so I kept working. Not only did I saw all those many, many branches off, I had to cart them down to a brush pile by the swamp. When contemplating and looking over the finished work, maybe the larger pines would have looked better with the lower branches still on. But all the smaller pines on the west side of the house looked nice, like a little park, especially when we mowed the lawn under them also. I am glad my dad had patience and did not get upset with me for doing that big project without asking for his go-ahead first. I just thought it was something that would help beautify and improve the looks of our yards and went ahead and did it.

BIRTHDAYS, HART
FAIR, HOMESICK

I have numerous fond memories of fun and enjoyable times during the summers. One delightful thing as a youngster was running through the spraying water from a hose. My mom would prop up the hose on something so the nozzle was the right height for us to run through the fine spray of water. As kids, we loved it and thought it was great fun! I used to do that summers for my children also, and I am sure many other mothers have done the same thing. There was one particularly hot day when it was too warm to do much of anything. My mom got a blanket for me to lie on outside to read and play. Then she set the sprinkler up with a fine mist not far away, blowing it my way and cooling me off. I thought that was pretty ingenious and very kind of her!

Another thoughtful and kind thing she did was try to make our birthdays a special day. She would always make us a delicious cake and fix a nice supper for us. We got to choose what we wanted her to fix for our birthday supper. I know I often chose her delicious breaded pork chops and baked potatoes. When our daughters were younger, we often let them choose a cheaper fast food restaurant as a special birthday treat. Sometimes I would let them choose a special meal for me to make for them. I know a couple of our daughters have kept up the tradition of letting the kids choose what they would like for their birthday supper.

Sometimes Darlene and I were able to stay at Aunt Emma's house for our birthdays which was a very memorable treat. It was great fun to go to the big city of Muskegon and stay all alone for a couple nights with Aunt Emma. To us farm girls, it was a big city! Muskegon is said to be the largest populated city on the western shores of Michigan. She would take us out to eat hamburgers, shakes, and fries that we never got otherwise! We went with her to the huge stores downtown and took our first rides in elevators and on escalators. Aunt Emma did not drive or have a car, so we would get around on the city bus. That was a lot of fun too, and a real experience for us farmers. We could catch the bus only a block from her house, so it was very convenient. She would play games with us or do puzzles; we had lots of fun. Aunt Emma owned her house, a big two-story home. She lived upstairs which had a big living area with two bedrooms, a large living room, and a large kitchen. Then, she rented out the downstairs which was also plenty big. Often, Christian school teachers knew about my aunt's apartment and would rent from her, so she had good renters. When I stayed at Aunt Emma's, she introduced me to toasted peanut butter and bacon sandwiches . . . so very delicious! I love them to this day and think of dear Aunt Emma when I am enjoying them.

Aunt Emma had enough money to do special things since she was single and worked many, many years at a factory, Sealed Power, in Muskegon. A thing I particularly remember about Aunt Emma is she liked keeping quite a bit of cash on hand in the house. She would hide one hundred dollar bills in large old Reader Digest condensed books on her shelves in the living room. We got a bunch of those Reader Digest books after Aunt Emma passed away. I looked very thoroughly through all of those old books hoping to find a one hundred dollar bill. I searched and searched; I shook them and shook them! Then after some time,

I went through them all again for a second and third time. I never found any hundred dollar bills! Either she remembered to remove them, or someone else found them and was very happy with their find.

Along that same note, when we moved into our older home in New Era, several antique pictures were left hanging on the walls. At one point, I took all the backs off of them to see if any previous owners had hid some money behind the pictures (like they sometimes did). Again, I did not find anything!

Aunt Emma often gave out large sums of money to her relatives on Christmas and always was very generous if my husband and I were going on a trip with our four daughters. She often gave us money to help out with expenses. Aunt Emma had a lot of good friends, and she went on some group tours with them—to Alaska and to Mexico. We always looked forward to her coming to stay at our house for a few days; she was such a nice, caring, and fun aunt.

When I was a teenager, Aunt Emma would have me come a week or more and help her houseclean. I had a good time when I stayed with her. I would work during the day washing walls and windows, cleaning cupboards, and many other things. She would pay me well for this. Then, evenings, we often did special things like go to a nice restaurant to eat our supper. One time she took me bowling with her and her friends. It was the first time I ever went bowling. I bowled four games and the last game I bowled three strikes in a row and wound up with a score of 180. That was something! After that, I really, really liked bowling and did a lot of it over the years. It was many years before I broke the record of that high score! It was always so much fun when my whole family was at my folks' house for a special occasion and someone suggested going bowling. I so enjoyed going with all my siblings and their spouses, and we would have a wonderful time together.

Now some assorted and varied short remembrances. First, I was very little when I was excited about the preacher coming for house visiting. I had a question I was anxious to ask him. My question was, "Where did God come from?" I guess he answered it satisfactorily for me at my very young age. I even remember the pastor's name, Rev. Van Oostenburg, but do not remember the elder that was with him.

I remember Mom taking time and wanting to hear all about our day at school when we got home, and sometimes we got fresh baked cookies then. Another thing about Mom, she was a good organizer and often would organize a family reunion with many people, and other types of get-togethers. Once, she had many neighbors and friends over for a fish fry and served it in the basement (with lots of extra tables and chairs set up).

My Dad enjoyed watching the birds. He had a hummingbird feeder, and in the winter had several boards with big long spikes that he could stick six to eight ears of corn on. He would set the boards on top of the snow, and the birds would come and eat the corn off the cobs. When thinking about my parents . . . they were good role models and always tried to do what was right. They strived to raise their children to do the same by going to church, doing their very best, being polite, respectful, learning by chores and work to be responsible, and to be content with what they had. And just like in any family . . . things were not always peaches and cream, but it is wonderful that you mainly just remember the good things!

I had a reputation in the neighborhood as the girl who did all the tractor driving. It just happened that way as Dad needed help, and I was the next oldest after the brothers were out of the house. I did most of the corn cultivating, as well as a good share of mowing the hay. Plus, I did a lot of raking the hay into windrows. I always was happy to do the tractor work.

Dad finally purchased a new New Holland baler so he could bale his own hay and not have to hire someone else with a baler to do it. Then, he got into custom baling and did a lot of it over the years. He was still working second shift at the factory in Muskegon, so many days he would get me started on the custom baling some place before he had to go to work. He would stay while I made a few rounds to make sure the baler was adjusted right according to the hay conditions. I knew how to make the adjustments but it was a little harder for me to figure out a good size and weight of the bale. I also had to know how to put in a new large roll of twine and knot it a certain way so the twine would feed through the machine. Sometimes, I would bale over half a day by myself, and then when my brother Don would get home from work, he would come and check on me to make sure things were going smoothly. If the bales needed an adjustment or if I had a breakdown, he could help out. I do not know what Dad got paid a bale for custom baling, but he paid me a cent a bale for doing the baling for him. That was plenty of pay in my estimation. Sometimes, on a real good day, we could average a thousand or more bales a day between several customers, so I would make a little money, and Dad needed to make some too.

My cousins, Darlene and I, and others in the county would participate in 4-H . . . which stands for Head, Heart, Hands, and Health. I went to 4-H many years and took up sewing, cooking, baking, vegetable gardening, and growing flowers. My mom taught cooking and baking; a neighbor by our school taught sewing. The only thing I did not like about sewing was there was a community 4-H program, and we had to model what we sewed whether it was just an apron, skirt, or dress. I did not like getting up in front! 4-H had many other projects you could participate in like drawing, painting, canning, quilting; also you could raise steers, pigs, sheep, goats, rabbits, chickens . . . to name a few. The Hart Fair always was the big occurrence in August before it was time to return to school. Those in 4-H and others could enter things they made at the fair with a chance to win some money and ribbons. I did enter various things a few years and got some ribbons.

We always really looked forward to going to the Hart Fair; it was a big community attraction. When we were younger, Dad always brought us. He enjoyed the fair, too, and liked looking around at the animals and visiting people he would run across. Dad liked watching the harness racing with the horses, and I did too. He would buy us a day pass so we could ride the rides as often as we wanted. Another thing, there used to be this tiny ice cream shop right on the corner by the fairgrounds. It was on the other side of the fenced-in grounds. We could still buy the cones through the fence, which we always did. They were soft serve, and they always made them so huge! We could hardly get the cones topped high with ice cream through the top part of the fence! It always was a fun thing to do.

When I was old enough to drive, the two cousins, Darlene, and I would go together to the fair. By going on a certain day, we only had to pay five dollars and could ride the rides all day, as many times as you wanted. Boy, did we go on the rides many, many times! We ran from ride to ride, and rode them over and over! We had a huge surprise when I was about seventeen. We were sitting in the bleachers watching something, and they had a drawing for a free girl's bike and a boy's bike. I sure was startled and astonished when I had the winning ticket for the girl's bike! It was so exciting and wonderful to have a brand new bike even though I was older. My old bike was not much at all. The bike I won was a very nice Schwinn, and it still is in the basement here at our house, so quite the antique.

Because I belonged to 4-H, I could attend 4-H camp on Stony Lake fourteen miles from our house. I was not really sure I wanted to do this and be away from home a whole week. But, a friend talked me into going; we were in the sixth or seventh grade. There were enough fun things to do during the day, but I remember being very homesick at night. My girlfriend had met some boys, and so she was not around to do things with me evenings. Since I was too shy, I did not make new friends there. I really had not been away from home all that much except to spend a night at a friend's occasionally.

Another time, my folks thought I would like to stay at my uncle Bill and aunt Helen's in Battle Creek for a couple of weeks (the uncle and aunt that later were in a car accident). He then was a manager at the huge Kellogg's Farm. Since they lived quite far away, I never even knew them that well. I think Dad thought I would like driving tractor for him some. I did this very little, and there was not a lot for me to do around there. I was so homesick nights! And of course, when I went to college, I was away from home and became homesick the first week. After that rough beginning I really enjoyed it, made wonderful friends, and it was an awesome experience. I know all these things are just a part of growing up and maturing us for when we are adults. We have to be able to face the good times and the bad times alike. I know, for me, when there are things I do not wish to do, it is just best to meet them head-on and get them over with.

After talking about being homesick, I recall a number of things that make me think of my home, and my enjoyment of growing up on the farm. First, I love the sounds of frogs because we could hear them croaking and singing nights in the swamp just beyond the barn. When I see an Allis Chalmers tractor or a New Holland baler, I think of our farm. The smell of burning leaves reminds me of home, since we often burned the leaves in the fall. For sure, always the smell of newly mowed grass or fresh mowed hay—more memories, and seeing black and white cows in the fields (Holsteins, like we owned). Breaded pork chops remind me of my special birthday suppers. Woodsmoke brings my thoughts back to when we heated with wood and coal, and the coziness and warmth. I so loved the lima beans which we grew in our garden, and so did my sister Darlene. Instead of maybe ice cream for an evening snack, Darlene and I liked buttered limas (I still do today). It seemed that pink peppermints were always the church candies! Pink peppermints remind me of how my mom would always have a fancy hanky prepared for church. In one corner she tied the peppermint, and in another corner her collection of coins for the offering plate.

I still remember our phone attached to the wall with a very long cord. We had a party line and the number was 754-11, so first a long ring and then a short. We could tell when some nosy neighbor was listening in on the party line. It would click when she picked up the receiver.

I recall how for quite awhile we had to wear our dresses all day on Sundays. Our parents felt it was a good way to keep us from being too boisterous and rambunctious on Sundays. For some time, we could not even ride our bikes on Sundays! Mom also would do all she could to prepare her nice Sunday dinner ahead on Saturdays. She would cook the roast on Saturday, peeled the potatoes and put them in cold water, and set them in the cellar way overnight (the cellar way is what we called a storage area off the kitchen, at the top of the basement steps). They did not want to do any more work than they absolutely had to on Sundays.

I sometimes cook a beef roast, potatoes, and carrots together like my mom often did. Then I mash those potatoes and carrots on my plate with a fork and spread on lots of butter. Very delicious! I especially remember Dad teaching us, at a young age, to play Pinochle and Pedro, since he enjoyed playing cards so much. Then some evenings Dad, Mom, Darlene, and I could play cards, mostly Pinochle. I think of Mom when I come in from outside drenched in sweat from working hard in our garden or in the yard, and run ice-cold water over my wrists. Mom taught us to do that when we were younger and needed to get cooled off from working outside. She said when we ran the cold water over our wrists, it would cool the blood down and then circulate, cooling us off faster. I think of Dad after he retired in 1965, how he continued to enjoy farming, working in the red pines, gardening, watching Tigers baseball on TV, playing Pinochle, and visiting. He was so good those years at chauffeuring widows and neighbors around when needed, and Mom would often ride along. If I bring a meal or baked goods to someone in need, I think of Mom who was often sending helpful dishes or some delicious freshly made desserts to others.

There was an elderly couple in our neighborhood living just beyond our 80 acres, a ways off the road in a secluded spot. My mom took it upon herself to check on them periodically, and Darlene and I often went along. Darlene remembers she and her friend, Mary, even brought their accordion and something similar to a keyboard along and played and sang for them. Walter Klydah was such a neat little man with a kind smile and a twinkle in his eyes. He and his wife lived on a very small plot of land with a tiny garden; the house was a dilapidated shack. Inside, things were old and rundown with kitchen, living room, and bedroom all in one room. I think Mrs. Klydah had some dementia. They were an interesting couple, not complainers, and seemed happy with the little they had. Mom liked to bring them nourishing food when she occasionally visited on account of her concern for them.

Knowing your neighbors, doing things with them, helping them, was a good opportunity to show Christ's love to others. I often mention about doing things with our second cousins. Their grandma lived up the road from them a half mile. She was also my dad's sister, Aunt Annie. Now she was an aunt with a real caring heart and totally unselfish about helping others! She somehow got acquainted with a man who was badly crippled and bedridden, living at the county-run nursing home in the area. Warren Gilbert could only listen to the radio, watch TV, and visit. He could not feed himself, read, or write since his hands and arms were too crippled. His head was bent close to his chest, and he could not move it. I do not believe he had family, and she felt sorry for him. She decided she would take care of him, and he agreed to come and live with her and Uncle John. What an undertaking that was for them, and what a way to show their Christian love. It pretty well tied them to staying at home, as I do not think he could have been left alone. Mr. Gilbert sure liked to talk, and if you would let him, he could talk steady for hours at a time! He liked having young people visit him (and liked to tell people I was his girlfriend), and when I was in my teens, I felt I should take time to visit him. I went up there every so often to sit and listen to him talk. He liked to go on and on about baseball games and almost any other topic. I hardly ever had to say a word. In fact, it was very difficult to get a word in at all—even to say it was time for me to go home!

I mention this story because of the big sacrifice for my aunt taking in this total stranger, and my mom too, when she took care of Grandpa Fischer for many years, until he passed away. Things were different back then, and people seemed to feel it was their obligation, and that they were accountable to care for parents and relatives. I am sure some of it could have been financial reasons also. I like the way the Amish take care of their parents by adding a smaller house for their parents to the existing home (a Dawdy Haus). I keep asking my children which one is going to add a Dawdy (means grandpa) Haus to their home for my husband and me when the time comes that we need assistance.

These last stories took place in the country, and my enjoyment of farms and country life is still in my blood after all these years. We live in the small town of New Era, but we can easily get to the country a half mile away in each direction. I like riding in the car through the country checking out crops and the farm sights. Also, my husband and I take rides through the countryside and through orchards near New Era on his restored tractors. He likes farming too, having helped a couple friends out a lot on their farms during his teenage and college years.

I think growing up on a farm helps you to be more aware of nature and God's creation. You are ready, after a hard day of work, to relax and take it easy. Maybe you learn to function at a better pace in life, not so hurried and always so rushed about. I know it happens to many—they get so busy at work, church, and school (all good things), but then have nothing left for family and that is not good! We always have to take time for our families. Do special little things with them and make good memories. Time keeps marching on so very fast! By the time you turn around a few times, you will have turned gray and likely be sitting in your recliners with your feet up remembering past memories. With each passing year, I appreciate more my spouse, family, health, and feel very content with what we have. The value you place on your home, on cars, large wardrobes, material things, prestige—-they become less and less important. Instead, God and things eternal become more and more valuable. They become priceless!

TRIPS, STUCK,
TEENAGER

We did not do a lot of traveling out of Michigan when growing up on the farm. I mentioned previously that my folks went to North Dakota, without us kids, to visit Dad's brother, wife, and nieces and nephews. Our little hundred and twenty acre farm must have seemed pretty small to them, since his nephew owned a farm with many cattle and over a thousand acres. This nephew and wife (my cousins) had eight children and were the friendliest group you would ever meet! Over the years, my husband, children, and I visited with them many times.

As a child, my first trip outside of Michigan was made possible by my aunt Emma. She took my mom, Darlene, and me to Milwaukee on our first plane ride. That was so much fun. I remember Darlene and I giggling when we would hit air pockets and had some bumps. We stayed in a huge hotel up on about the twelfth floor (and it was so noisy since they were working on the sidewalks with jackhammers), saw the movie *Around the World in 80 Days,* took in the Milwaukee Zoo for a day, and went out to eat many times. It was a neat experience for us grade-schoolers. Aunt Emma provided these special excursions for a lot of her nieces and nephews. My brother Herb and two cousins went overnight to Chicago. He said they went by train, stayed in a hotel, and then flew back.

Another trip, when we were teenagers, was when my brother Don and his wife took Darlene and me along with them and their two children, to see all the cousins in North Dakota. We stayed with them on the huge farm I mentioned earlier. If I remember right, their eight children were all still at home at the time. There sure was a lot of lively chatter and conversation around their huge table at meal times. They lived on a dirt road and had only one close neighbor across the road. With the farms so huge and neighbors spread out, every time a vehicle drove by many kids would jump up and look out the windows to see who was going by, something I thought rather funny. It seemed to be the entertainment of the day. One night they wanted to do something special for us, so they took us swimming. We thought that sounded like fun, so we piled in the vehicles and drove over to this little lake in the middle of a fenced-in cow pasture. I did not enjoy swimming much as every time I took a step on the muddy bottom of the lake, I thought it was likely a cow plop! To these cousins, though, who had no Lake Michigan or Fogg Lake, it was a place to swim. The meals my cousin Betty could spread out on the table were something else. With their own beef, garden produce, and her love of baking—they were wonderful and bountiful meals!

One other trip we took was with Dad and Mom for a few days to Chicago. Darlene was a teenager and I was maybe in college. We stayed at the good friend of Dad and Mom's whom they had us call Aunt Tillie. She lived in a really neat old house with quite a few special antiques. We did many fun things while there—-took the train downtown, rode the elevator to the top of the forty-story Prudential Building, drove to O'Hare Airport and watched airplanes, ate at the O'Hare Oasis over the expressway, and went to the Field Museum of Natural History. That was our first taste of the big city of Chicago. Later on my husband and I, and our children often drove to Chicago for a day to see the sights.

I have completed my stories of my younger years, so now some from when I was a teenager. I mentioned our bus rides to the high school in Montague, fourteen miles away. They were quite long rides by the time all the kids were picked up and dropped off again on the way home from school. We were some of the last kids still on the bus when returning home. I told how sometimes we had lots of snow to get through with the bus, but this one time we had dirt and sand to get through. We had always lived on a dirt road until about 1960, when they decided to pave the first three miles of Arthur Road. They had started this process with the grading, and bringing in fill dirt. Consequently, it was necessary for the bus to go through when the road was full of loose and deep sand. Well, finally this one afternoon on the way home, the bus could not make it and got stuck! The road construction crew had already quit for the day. There we sat—no cell phones to call for assistance. Would the bus driver have to send an older kid to a house miles down the road to call for help, or what? Well, this farmer's teenage boy noticed the bulldozer sitting there. He said he knew how to run one of those and actually got it started, and used it to push out the bus! I am surprised the bus driver allowed him to just use it like that, but we all were glad we got out and could get home, and not have to sit there for hours and hours stranded. I remember someone composed a note and addressed it to the road crew, left it fastened to the seat of the bulldozer, and thanked them for the use of their equipment to push out the school bus!

The second story also happened on the bus ride home. The Fischers (my uncle and aunt) had a man, George Keller, who worked for them some. He stayed in a house my uncle and aunt had back a ways on their property. Sometimes they could get a lot of good work out of him, and sometimes he would get drunk and would not come to work for days. I think they felt sorry for him, so just used him when they could; he was a nice enough man who had a bad drinking problem. We knew him, too, since we worked with him sometimes. George would often walk to the Rothbury tavern six miles away when he had the money to buy some drinks. Our bus driver would see him walking, sometimes, and would give him a ride on the bus. He picked George up one afternoon and he was very tipsy, and had a bottle of something sticking out of his back pocket. He staggered up the steps, wobbled down the aisle, and was happy to see me and chose to sit beside me. I think my face turned red and I was rather mortified, but I still tried to be polite to him. The bus driver kept watching in the rear-view mirror to make sure George behaved himself. He did okay except he talked rather loudly.

For those teenage and high school years, the popular fads were convertible cars, guys wearing sports jackets with the letters of the sports on them, and letting the girls wear the jackets or their class rings if they went steady. Girls wore pullover sweaters, pleated skirts, and a lot of straight skirts (no shorter than the knee). Also, tennis shoes, bobby socks, and high heels were in for the girls. Guys did not have any butch hair cuts but longer, combed hair, and neat. Girls' hair was often curly and styled. Plaid skirts for girls and plaid sport coats for the guys were popular. Plus, guys wore tight fitted dark jeans. I did not have a closet full of clothes. It seems like I would wear a different outfit each day of the week, and then needed to repeat those same outfits the following week. We almost always got a new hat for church for Easter. There was one lady in our church who had a vast collection of fancy hats, large ones and very colorful. It was not good to sit behind her in church with her very large hats! It seemed like she wore a different hat every Sunday, so we always watched to see what hat Mavis was wearing to church. Or we would sit behind the lady who wore a mink stole and this little critter's tiny head with beady little eyes, nose, also feet and tail all were still on the stole. We could not help but stare at that little critter! In fact, there was one mink on back of the collar and two more mink on front. The lady's brother-in-law in New Era actually owned a mink farm. I recall Dad and I stopped there once and saw all the mink in many cages. This got me thinking, so I telephoned the lady from church (I visit her occasionally) and asked her a few questions. They shipped the pelts to New York. She stated they were nasty little animals, had very sharp teeth, and would bite. Sometimes horses were slaughtered for meat for the mink. Mink have a terrible odor and people had to be very careful when cutting the hides off not to hit the stinky scent glands. I remember opening our corncrib door once and there was a big black stinky animal that scared me. I thought maybe it was a mink or it also could have been a muskrat or a weasel (all of these can be found in Michigan). Mink come in different colors . . . dark, dark black, a pretty chocolate brown, beautiful gray, and some albino white ones. The meat was not usable but the fat could be made into a good lotion for softer hands. A company would buy that, add a perfume to it, and make the lotion. This lady said she still had her mink stole in her closet until a couple months ago. A relative asked about it and wondered if he could have it, so she let him take it. Fur coats were in back then and even my mom owned one that was so silky and soft. We liked sitting next to her in church when she wore it. This coat lasted her for years and years, and then she finally had it made into a three-quarters length coat and still wore it.

It seemed like my first two years of high school, I was always studying and trying to get good grades. By my junior and senior years, I started having more fun and did not always just study. I was too shy, however, to participate in class and sometimes got marked down on report cards because of it. I did not do sports when in high school. I would have liked to have played girls' basketball, but could not because the practice was after school, thus, a problem for getting home. The popular things to do were go to movies, dances, listen to rock and roll on the radio, cruise around in cars, hang out with your friends, participate in school activities, attend the prom, and watch the basketball and football games. I, however, did not participate in much of the above except I did things with my friends, attended the church functions, and we liked going to football games. Football was by far the most popular sport then, and both of my brothers played the game. They even ran a spectator bus to the away football games that you could sign up to ride for fifty cents.

I was not one of the popular kids in high school and for me, it certainly did not matter. I had many good friends and we had fun times. Once I got my driver's license, my parents were very good about letting me use their car. I remember filling the car with friends several times and driving north of Pentwater (twenty-six or so miles away) to a place called King's Canyon. My brother, Don, and his wife first showed us this spot. You drove up to this very high bluff over Lake Michigan. Then, there was a canyon, and we liked climbing down it to the lake. It was quite difficult to make the climb back up to the top! Often you had to grab a straggly tiny plant or bush to pull yourself up in the steepest places. But it was fun and a pretty spot. Later, between 1969 and 1973, they built the Ludington Pumped Storage Plant just north of this canyon. This is a hydroelectric plant and reservoir jointly owned by Consumers Energy and DTE Energy. We have not been back for many years to see if the canyon is still there. It probably is, but I am sure it would be overgrown with brush and trees.

Like most new drivers, I liked to drive whenever I got a chance, I always wanted to drive to catechism and Young Peoples' Society at our church in New Era on Wednesday nights. The preacher, Rev. DeVries, was very good at expounding the catechism, and he made it very interesting. I did not like to miss. We did some fun things in Young Peoples too, like going to Chicago to hear Billy Graham. Anyway, one Wednesday night it was rather blustery. Dad, knowing I was an inexperienced driver on snowy roads, said I should stay home from attending catechism. I coaxed and pleaded until he finally said okay. All went well on the way to church, but the storm had picked up in intensity as I headed home. Two miles into the trip there were huge snow drifts all the way across the road. I stepped on the gas hoping to make it through, but did not, and got stuck. Now I was worried—-boy, would Dad be upset when I would have to call him for help (I was near a house on the corner). I sat there pondering about my predicament knowing Dad would be angry about having to come out in the storm, especially since he did not want me driving in the bad weather in the first place! All of a sudden, I noticed some lights by the corner house, and yippee, a tractor started coming in my direction to help me out. It was someone from our church, and he pulled me through the drifts with the tractor and a chain. I sure was thankful to Mr. Pranger! To show my appreciation, I baked him some cookies and brought them over to him the next day. I do not remember if I told Dad about getting stuck, but I must have. A lesson learned: parents do often know best!

I am thankful our parents were good role models; that they raised us in the Christian faith and taught us the importance of faithful church attendance. We learned God is to be trusted and obeyed, and He gives us blessings over and over. He is an awesome God, a righteous God, and the Creator and Ruler over the universe. They showed us by doing how to persevere and always do a good day's work.

I graduated from high school in 1962. I got tired of people always asking what I wanted to do after I graduated because I did not know. I did not want to be a secretary, nurse, or teacher and there did not seem to be as many options back then. Not all young ladies even went on to college or sought a career. Many got married right out of high school. I wanted to be a wife and mother, and that is all I ever desired to be. I did go on to college in Grand Rapids and still came home summers to stay on the farm. There was always plenty of work to help out with at home, and jobs at neighbors where I could earn money for attending college.

22 RIFLE, LATER YEARS, DREAMS COME TRUE

As I look back on all the recollections and stories of my early and teenage years on our small farm, I now feel the need to briefly tie the "back then" with the "present." I did go on to college, the Grand Rapids School of the Bible and Music and graduated in 1966.

I have one last story that happened during my college years. A girlfriend from college was staying with me on the farm for a couple nights, and we came home from an outing. My folks were gone so we had to walk into the dark house. We proceeded into the house, turned on the lights, were relaxing a bit and about ready to prepare for bed. All of a sudden, we heard what sounded just like footsteps up in the attic. We both heard them and really got scared! I was aware that my dad kept a loaded 22 rifle in their bedroom closet, and I knew how to shoot it having done some target practice with it. I quickly grabbed the gun, and we both made a beeline for the bathroom where we could lock ourselves in. This was not a very comfortable place to wait because it was a small bathroom. But wait we did, sitting on the toilet seat and on the tub, shaking in fright, with me holding the gun. We were much too scared and too chicken to go out of the bathroom to see if someone was in the house. We sat there and waited and waited. It was a terribly long time . . . at least an hour. Later, when Dad and Mom came in and we explained what was going on, Dad went up and thoroughly searched the attic. I do not think he really thought there was someone up there, but for our peace of mind, he checked it out. He knew that sometimes the old house had a tendency to do some creaking and groaning, especially if it was a windy day. There was no one up there so we felt rather foolish. But it sure did sound like footsteps, and I will say today, that we were surely convinced that someone was up there walking around!

The very first car I owned was a Ford Fairlane, about a 1959, when I was in my third year of college. Dad helped me buy it for five hundred dollars. It sure made getting home from college on weekends much easier. Prior to owning a car, I had to walk to downtown Grand Rapids, maybe eight blocks, carrying my heavy suitcase to catch a bus home. Then my parents often would have to bring me back to the dorms on Sunday evenings. Sometimes, I could catch a ride with a girlfriend. Other times, I rode with a young man who was preaching and ministering at a chapel near our farm and going to a different college in Grand Rapids. I did not go home that often, though, during the semesters. There were always a lot of fun activities and basketball games to attend while at college.

My second car I bought myself after working at St. Mary's Hospital and saving some money. It was a 1964 Chevy Impala and I paid $1,025 for it in cash. It was a great car and even made a trip to California and back. I still owned it when I got married, and we used it for a second car for some time.

After graduating from college, I stayed on in the dorms for another two years, and was a dorm mom while I worked full time at St. Mary's Hospital as a desk clerk. Meanwhile, a girlfriend and I started planning an adventure to take a big trip across the United States, seeing the sights and moving to California. First, we worked at a canning company the summer before we left and stayed on the farm with my folks. We needed to earn some extra money for the big trip. That summer I had one date with the plant manager (who later became my husband), and then we left for California. Neither of us had traveled much, so we took in a lot of sights on our way to California, and we were on the road for two and a half weeks. We located near Los Angeles, two blocks from my friend's uncle and family, and found a very nice, furnished apartment. The apartment had a pool and a beautiful view of the foothills not far away. There were only ten apartments in the complex, and we often had the pool to ourselves. We both found work right away at a small hospital just across the street. I worked in the surgery department, and my friend in the cafeteria. I brought people in for their surgeries on the gurneys and cleaned and autoclaved the surgical instruments, putting them in the packs in perfect order for the next surgery. We enjoyed seeing many sights, attractions, and the beauty of California. We had fun spending time with her uncle and family, went to their church where he was the pastor, and lived there almost two years. But then we started missing family and the happenings back home too much, and decided to head back to Michigan.

Next, I lived in Grand Rapids again and worked at Amway close by. The best thing that happened during this time was that I started dating the young man I had the one date with before leaving Michigan. Most weekends I went home and stayed on the farm with my parents rather than staying in the city, and could date Dick then too. We had grown up not far from each other in the country but hung around with different young people. To me, it was astonishing and amazing that I had a dream of getting married while in California. When I started walking down the aisle and focused on my husband to be, who was standing there waiting for me but Richard P. Walhout! No one can say that dreams do not come true, as Dick and I were married June 2, 1973. To us, it was all God's plan that we both remained single, and after returning to Michigan we started dating and fell in love. We have been very happily married for forty-six years. God has been good! He answers prayers! I have mentioned our daughters, and we raised four of them. Visiting Grandma and Grandpa Kuipers on the farm and having them babysit was very much a part of their lives when growing up, as was the presence of their Grandma and Grandpa Walhout.

My parents have been gone for some time now. Dad passed away first in June of 1987 when he was eighty-four years old. It was unexpected because until then he had been doing fine physically. One evening he had to have emergency surgery, and they found out he had colon cancer. It had also spread into several lymph nodes. He recuperated from the surgery and went home for a couple weeks, but he then started having heart problems. So he spent more nights in the hospital and had more tests. I had been spending time with him when I could at the hospital, but in the afternoon before they were going to let him go home, I worked in his garden. His pride and joy was his garden, and I knew he would feel disappointed seeing it so full of weeds. The plans were to discharge him the next day. Later that afternoon, before supper, he passed away in the hospital due to a heart attack. I always felt like I did not get to say my final good-bye to him. If I had known what was going to happen, I certainly would have spent those final hours with him rather than pulling weeds to make his garden look presentable. I always felt bad about that. Now I always try to say good-bye to my husband properly when he goes away someplace, or to my children too, when they have been visiting us.

Mom passed away in a convalescent home in 1998, one month after her 90th Birthday. We kept her in her own home as long as we possibly could, but she had dementia and started needing more care. That was very hard for me to have her put in a nursing home. When that day came, I had my brother and sister-in-law bring her to the home. With her dementia, however, after a few weeks she could hardly even remember her own home of so many years. I distinctly remember her last day on this earth. The home called the family and told us her time of death was probably near. I went up right after my morning bus run and spent the day with her as well as other family members. She was conscious, but did not talk. I could have called the school to be excused from my afternoon bus run, but I decided to go ahead and do it being there was not much I could do for Mom. Others from the family were staying with Mom, so she was not alone. I planned to return after the bus run. I recall I had dropped most of the kids off and specifically remember who I had just dropped off and where I was turning when I felt very strongly in my heart that my mom had just passed away. When I returned home from driving bus, I had a phone call telling me Mom passed away at the very time I had felt she did. I feel there are times when there are very special bonds between a mom and a daughter. I have felt those close ties and bonds with my own daughters in certain incidents and happenings.

I was thinking of my parents, my siblings, and the farm as I went on a tractor ride this evening. I went through the apple orchards now laden with beautiful red delicious apples, enjoyed rolling countryside, and watched the sky getting brilliant as the sun was starting to go down. I enjoyed the smell of freshly mowed grass just as I enjoyed the smell of freshly mowed hay when growing up. It was beautiful to see the asparagus fern blowing in the breeze and having that breeze blowing on my face——and smelling the fresh air. It made me feel like "I was back in the saddle again" driving the tractor from my growing up days on the farm. I think all my tractor driving and pulling lengthy equipment was good experience for bus driving. I became a bus driver after marriage. When I first was licensed, I drove for a public school for two years. Next, I was a stay-at-home mom and raised our four daughters. After all the girls were attending New Era Christian School, a bus driving position opened up there, and I drove bus for that school for twenty-three years! That was a way for us to help put the children through Christian education (which was a priority for us) and for them to go to Christian colleges. Also, it was a way to help out the schools that were so valuable to us in educating our children.

After just finishing reading a book today about all the problems two people had when their five children went astray, I am thankful again for a good Christian upbringing. And I am thankful too, that we could provide it for our children in our home, through our church, through our Christian schools, and with the help of Christian grandparents. In the world we live in today, we need all the help we can get when raising our children. There are many temptations for kids, and it is so important we make sure we know where our children are, who they hang around with, where their interests lie, and keep the lines of communication open between them and us as parents. The famous radio host, author, and Christian psychologist, Dr. James Dobson, writes about passing on our faith in his book *Your Legacy, The Greatest Gift.* He talks about how the most important thing we can do in life as parents is to pass on the baton of faith and our Christian heritage on to our children, and them to pass the baton of faith on to their children, and again to the children of the next generations. What more important thing do we have to do on this earth than to make sure our children accept Christ, put their faith in Him, and go to heaven someday? When you see many empty pews in churches today, does that mean the batons are not being passed on . . . are being fumbled and dropped? I certainly hope not!

The things I cherish most in life are foremost my husband and family, and our Christian heritage which we are part of through both sides of our families. When growing up on the farm, I loved being around family and the good family times together. Then, when raising our own family, again I valued our times together, uniting us and bonding us! Now we are so glad when we as grandparents can bond with our ten treasured grandchildren. We still live in the large, two-story home in New Era, Michigan where we have lived since first married. The whole family gets together occasionally to have fun, fellowship, and make new memories. It is very interesting indeed when we pack so many in the house and need to share just one bathroom. Some of the family now lives in Texas, some in South Dakota, and two families about an hour away, so we certainly relish and appreciate the family times together.

To tie things up, I would like to include some final thoughts. Bad things happen in the world, and life can be so difficult sometimes. It seems some prayers go unanswered, tragedy happens, there is suffering, pain; we are overcome with sadness, things seem unfair, there is cruelty, doubts, despair, but we have to "press on." We need to remember that God is always in control, and God is good! We, in our finite minds, cannot see the whole picture. We need faith, assurance, and hope in God to carry us on and see us through! There will come a day when Christians will have answers to their questions and see the whole completed picture!

How wonderful to know that God is always near. He is there in the brilliant sunrise and in the splendor of the sunset. He is there in a bird's glad song, in the rippling grass, in a wind's soft whisper or in a mighty storm; and He is with a person in their life and in their heart! The relevance and significance of the family has come through a lot in this book, so take time to enjoy your family, and teach them about God. Play with them, work with them, talk and walk with them, share with them, take trips with them, love them, and bond with them. Children need to feel loved and feel secure. The child-rearing time in your life will go so fast, and your children will soon be leaving your nest. Show by example how to be happy and content with the little things. Do not let them get attached to costly things that the world seems to think are important. Teach your children how to be responsible, how to work hard and put in a good day's work, to have integrity, be honorable, moral, and upright. So many today are having a very difficult time finding people who are willing to work, or those who know how to work, and how to work conscientiously. Not everyone can grow up on a farm, but we did learn how to work there. Kids can build good work ethics by helping at home too, by taking on small jobs after school, or by obtaining jobs during their teenage years.

My stories and thoughts are completed! I have mentioned many things that were important to me in life as I was growing up. I hope some of these things will make sense to others and be helpful on their life's journey. My earnest prayer is that what I have written will be delightful, engaging, captivating, appealing, and beneficial to others. I am so thankful now to have my stories and memories in a book so my spouse, children, sons-in-law, grandchildren, extended family, friends, neighbors, and hopefully many others will savor and delight in reading *A Farm Girl's Memories*.

Aunt Emma and Mom (sisters)

Uncle Henry and Aunt Dorothy

Uncle Bill and Aunt Helen

Uncle Pat and Aunt Min

Family Picture, Darlene About 8, Judy 12, & Herb 15

Cousin Carl, Dad and Mom

Mom's Array of Saturday Baked Goods!

Dad & Mom in Their Early 70s (maybe 1975)

Siblings– From Left, Judy, Don, Herb, Elinor, & Darlene (1987)

Dick and Judy's Wedding, June 2, 1973

Dick and Judy's Home in New Era

Walhout girls, Ages 2, 4, 6, and 8

BIBLIOGRAPHY

Dobson, Dr. James, <u>Your Legacy, The Greatest Gift</u>, Chapter Two, The Second Generation, pp 5 - 6, Copyright 2014 by Siggie, LLC: FaithWords Hachette Book Group.

Though I did not quote Dr. Dobson directly in my book, I mention his idea about the passing of the baton of faith from generation to generation in my last chapter. This idea about the baton is in his book <u>Your Legacy,</u> so I included the two paragraphs below where he mentions it.

"If you have ever watched track and field competition, you know that relay races are usually won or lost in the transfer of the baton. A runner rarely drops the prize on the backside of the track. The critical moment occurs when he burns around the final turn and prepares to hand the baton to the next runner. If either of them has fumble-fingers and fails to complete a secure pass, their team usually loses.

So it is with the Christian life. When members of one generation are committed to the Gospel of Jesus Christ and are determined to finish strong, they rarely fumble the baton. But getting the handoff securely in the hands of children can be difficult and risky. That is when Christian commitments between generations can be dropped. It isn't always the fault of the parents. Some young runners refuse to reach out and grasp the baton. Either way, there is nothing more tragic than failing to transfer the baton to those who come after."

I got permission to mention about the baton of faith from Dr. James Dobson's Family Talk. The assistant to Dr. Dobson called me on 11/13/19 granting me permission and gave me the name of the book where Dr. Dobson talks about the idea.

A NOTE FROM THE AUTHOR

I wanted to include this note and say it has meant a lot to me to have accomplished writing a book. I did not think I could do it as felt inadequate, but I was willing to give it my very best effort. It has been a long process, but I faithfully stuck with it, and it most definitely is a rewarding and fulfilling achievement. I started writing on April 23, 2019 and my goal was to get it done and published in 2020. I think 2020 has a nice sound to it so wanted that year as my copyright date. I am finishing it this week and plan to send the completed manuscript off tomorrow, on May 7, 2020. This makes me feel elated and very eager to get the printing process underway.

I have had a lot of time to work on it of late with the "stay at home" mandates because of the coronavirus. Who would ever have thought that 2020 would go down in history as the year of the terrible COVID-19 pandemic. It is such a tragedy with so many deaths . . . what a sad and frightening thing! When entering 2020, little did we know that we would become familiar with such things as social distancing, having to stay at home so much, and needing to wear masks when going to stores and to other public places. We hope and pray that the world will again soon return to a more normal and prosperous life.

Though this was not included in my book, I did wish to make mention about the virus as such a different and difficult life we are facing yet in May of 2020!

One more thing . . . if you enjoyed reading my first book ever, I would love to hear from you. My email address is tennisjaw@ gmail.com. You are welcome to send me an email and I thank you very much, Judith Kuipers Walhout

ABOUT THE AUTHOR

A Farm Girl's Memories is the first book Judith has written. She and her husband of 46 years reside in an older two-story home in New Era, Michigan. It is located right by the downtown area and overlooks all the happenings in this little town. New Era is a quaint small town with under 500 in population. There is even a siren that blows every night at 6 p.m. It used to signal quitting time at the local canning company. Now when the grandchildren are visiting, they tell them the whistle blows announcing it is supper time. New Era is located in Oceana County which is famous for asparagus and is called the "Asparagus Capital of the World."

This over 120 year old home in New Era is located five miles from the farm where Judith grew up. Since the town is small and friendly, it was a wonderful, safe place to raise a family. Dick and Judith like living in a small town, but they can still enjoy the country a half mile away in each direction from New Era. They often drive by the farm where she grew up, where all the fond memories told about in her new book occurred.

Now seventy-five years of age, Judith is retired from driving school bus for twenty-five years. She totally enjoys retired life and does a lot of reading, rides bike, likes jigsaw puzzles, plays Scrabble, bowls, plays pickle ball, goes on tractor rides with her husband, gardens and does yard work, snowmobiles, and enjoys watching professional tennis. Her favorite player is Roger Federer and she has his autograph from a tennis tournament she attended.

She also likes to keep in contact with her four daughters by emailing them almost every day. Dick and Judith treasure family visits and get-togethers, and love spending time with their ten grandchildren whenever possible. With a family in Texas and one in South Dakota, it makes times together a bit more difficult.

Thank you for choosing *A Farm Girl's Memories* to read. Judith's faith in God is a priority in her life and she hopes that comes through in her book. We hope you enjoy the happenings on the farm and relish and delight in the stories included.